R. SCOTT REBER, CFP®, MBA

LOVE

How to talk to
your partner about
money and not kill
each other

FINANCE

Love and Finance
How To Talk to Your Partner About Money and Not Kill Each Other
R. Scott Reber, CFP®, MBA

Securities Disclosure

Securities are offered through LPL Financial, Member FINRA/SIPC. Reber Investments is another business name of Independent Advisor Alliance, LLC. All investment advice is offered through Independent Advisor Alliance, LLC, a registered investment advisor. Independent Advisor Alliance, LLC is a separate entity from LPL Financial.

The content is developed from sources believed to be providing accurate information. The information in this material is not intended as tax or legal advice. Please consult legal or tax professionals for specific information regarding your individual situation. The opinions expressed and material provided are for general information and should not be considered a solicitation for the purchase or sale of any security.

Limit of Liability/Disclaimer of Warranty: While the publisher and author have used their best efforts in preparing this book, they make no representations of warranties with respect o the accuracy or completeness of the contents of this book and specifically disclaim any implied warranties of merchantability of fitness for a particular purpose. No warranty may be created or extended by sales representatives or written sales materials. The advice and strategies contained herein may not be suitable for your situation. You should consult with a professional where appropriate. Neither the publisher nor author shall be liable for any loss of profit or any other commercial damages, including but not limited to special, incidental, consequential or other damages.

This publication is designed to provide accurate and authoritative information in regard to the subject matter covered. It is sold with the understanding that the publisher is not engaged in rendering legal, accounting, investing, or other professional services. If you require legal advice or other expert assistance, you should seek the services of a competent professional.

Printed in the United States.

Cover and book design by Asya Blue Design.

ISBN 979-8-9926242-1-2 Paperback
ISBN 979-8-9926242-2-9 Hardcover
ISBN 979-8-9926242-0-5 Ebook

To contact the author, visit:
www.reberinvestments.com
Scott@reberinvestments.com

Dedicated to my mother Donna, the best at sarcastic comments, which provided endless inspiration for this book's witty dialogue.

Why I wrote this book

The conversation began with a simple question, innocuous enough on its own: "Do you think we should start saving for our retirement?"

But as soon as the words left her mouth, Sarah felt the tension in the room thicken like a soupy fog. She knew her husband's attitude toward money—he was a spender, a man who saw each paycheck as an opportunity to indulge in the finer things in life. She, on the other hand, was more cautious, more practical. She saw money as a means to an end—a future free from worry and financial insecurity.

Her husband's answer confirmed her fears: "Why save for something that may never come? Let's live in the moment and enjoy what we have now."

Sarah's heart sank. This wasn't the first time she and her husband had clashed over their finances. She couldn't help but feel like they were on different planets. She loved her husband, but it seemed they were fundamentally incompatible when it came to money, unable to communicate about something that was so vital to their future.

She wanted to continue the conversation, but her words seemed to get stuck in her throat. The uncomfortable silence between them stretched on, punctuated only by the sound of the clock ticking on the wall.

Finally, Sarah let out a resigned sigh. There was no use trying to convince him, she thought. It was easier to just keep the peace and let him have his way. But deep down, she couldn't shake off the unease that came with avoiding such an important topic. They may have been able to ignore their financial differences for now, but she knew that, eventually, those differences would catch up with them. And when they did, they would be much harder to reconcile.

My role as an advisor

As a financial advisor, my profession is not merely about handling the intricacies of numerical figures and fiscal reports. It extends to managing the complex emotional landscapes that are inevitably intertwined with the tangible aspects of people's finances. Every day, I am confronted with a scenario that has become all too familiar to me: a couple seated across from me at my office or a coffee shop, their faces etched with a cocktail of emotions—discomfort, frustration, fear, and uncertainty. Their physical expressions say it all, with their clenched hands, lack of eye contact, and tense silences, clear indicators of an impending conflict and the inevitable conversation about finances making us all uneasy.

Each discussion delves into the depths of the couple's financial habits and beliefs, dissecting how their money should be managed, spent, and invested for an uncertain future. The idea of planning for a future that feels so distant is often overwhelming for them; it brings to the surface insecurities, differences of opinion, and deeply ingrained behaviors toward money.

Regrettably, this struggle with money-related conversations is not an isolated case. It is a very common issue that has haunted my professional life, an unwelcome menace looming over every meeting. Each time I found myself seated opposite another couple embroiled in this heated debate, I could feel a sense of frustration gnawing at me. I'd often find myself thinking, "How can I devise a comprehensive financial plan for them when they can't even hold a civil conversation about money?" Each couple's conflicting views on saving and spending mirrored their inability to find common ground, making my job exponentially more challenging.

I was acutely aware that money was a delicate subject for most people. It wasn't just about numbers or balance sheets; it was deeply personal and had profound emotional implications. However, as someone who had chosen the path of financial advising, I also knew that open dialogue was crucial for any successful financial strategy. How I wished more couples would acknowledge this fundamental truth!

I had witnessed how the inability to communicate about money could strain even the strongest of relationships. It could erect invisible walls between partners, making it increasingly difficult for them to express their fears, dreams, and aspirations effectively. I understood that money held immense personal value, often encompassing a person's past experiences and emotional baggage. It was a window into their true self; money revealed the true intentions of their heart.

And yet, as a financial advisor, I had an unspoken duty to help couples navigate through this labyrinth of emotions and financial jargon. So, to better serve my clients and alleviate some of my own professional challenges, I decided to explore the underlying psychology of why discussing money was such a daunting task for couples. What deep-seated issues did this topic unearth? Why would a couple who seemed like soulmates in every other aspect of their lives find it so difficult to talk about their finances?

I embarked on a journey into the human psyche, immersing myself in research and studies about money-related behaviors.

Although I am no psychologist, what I discovered was akin to uncovering a buried treasure.

As I dug deeper into the psychology of money, I realized that it was a complex and multifaceted topic. It involved not just beliefs and values but also deep-rooted emotions and behaviors that were often shaped by our upbringing and past experiences.

Armed with this newfound knowledge, I found myself better equipped to guide my clients. I helped them understand their own attitudes toward money, identify the emotional triggers they associated with it, and comprehend how these emotions affected their communication with their partner. This mutual understanding improved each couple's conversations about finances, preventing potential conflicts and strengthening their connection. As a result, I have become more than just a financial advisor; I now also facilitate healthier relationships and better communication, not by choice but out of necessity.

My goal in writing this book is to pass on what I have learned and seen work with other couples, as well as within my own marriage. I believe that by sharing these insights, stories, and strategies, I can help couples develop healthier relationships and stronger communication skills.

Our exploration of effective communication will not just scratch the surface. We will delve deeply into its different elements, from our own values and beliefs to gaining a better understanding of our partner's fears and inner workings. We will discover how communication can bridge gaps or erect barriers and learn to wield it as a powerful tool to strengthen our personal relationships.

Once we've thoroughly examined and mastered the pillars of effective communication, covering not only spoken and written language but also the subtle nuances of body language and tone,

I plan to transition our focus toward the intricacies and best practices of personal financial management. This will encompass understanding the foundational principles of budgeting, saving, investing, and managing debt, with the goal of achieving financial stability and independence.

We'll unravel the secrets behind managing money wisely, learning not just about numbers and calculations but also about the importance of financial discipline and planning. We'll debunk myths surrounding budgeting and debt management, providing you with practical strategies that can be tailored to suit your individual financial goals.

Consider this journey akin to staring at a beautiful landscape painting. At first glance, you see the broad strokes—the mountains, the rivers, and the skies. But as you look more closely, you start noticing the fine details—the play of light and shadow, the subtle color gradations, the texture of the brush strokes. That's what our exploration will be like: moving from understanding the broad concepts to appreciating their finer details and nuances.

By intertwining these two seemingly disparate topics—communication and finance—I will equip you with skills that are not just beneficial but essential for navigating through life's diverse challenges. I hope this is not simply sharing information; it's an opportunity to actively participate in a life-changing learning adventure.

Some clarifications

While my target audience is married couples, anyone can benefit from the information presented (whether single, cohabiting, newlyweds, newly engaged, divorced, or remarried).

I will be using the terms "spouse," "mate," and "partner "interchangeably.

In terms of gender, there are ongoing discussions surrounding this topic today, such as "Is gender a social construct?" However, that is not the focus of this book. I am examining how communication and potential conflicts arise between two individuals in a relationship regardless of their gender.

Additionally, my focus will be on the average couple and not extreme cases of dysfunctional relationships or dysfunctional money management.

CONTENTS

CHAPTER 1

INTRODUCTION

You probably know a couple like my clients Simon and Michelle.

They'd been married ten years and had two children, ages eight and ten, both athletes. Both parents had good jobs: Simon was a lead engineer for a NASCAR team based in Mooresville, NC, while Michelle had just gone back to work part-time as a medical assistant, since both kids were now old enough not to strangle each other if left alone.

The first time they sat across my desk from me, I asked them the introductory questions I ask all my clients. These initial questions are crucial for building trust, understanding their financial situation, and setting the foundation for effective financial planning. I try to use open-ended questions to encourage them to share detailed information about their financial goals, concerns, and personal circumstances, like: "What are your current financial concerns?" "What are your short- and long-term financial goals?" and "What do you hope to gain from financial planning?" (1)

At first, Simon and Michelle stared at me like two deer in the headlights, and then stared at each other, not knowing what to say.

As a licensed Financial Advisor, CERTIFED FINANCIAL PLANNER™ (2), and managing director of Reber Investments, I specialize in helping my clients build long-term financial plans. Simon and Michelle's shocked expressions didn't surprise me at all! Many couples, no matter how rich or poor they are, have never really talked to each other about their finances. They often don't know how much they spend, how much debt they have, or even how much money they have.

After years of watching couples struggle with, ignore, or even argue about their finances, I realized that the foundation of any successful financial plan is successful communication.

This book provides couples with the tools and knowledge to change their personal money conversations. Talking about money doesn't have to be a fight. It doesn't have to cause resentment, fear, or anxiety. Talking about money can—and should!—be a way for couples to strengthen their relationship for long-term happiness and prosperity.

At the beginning of our marriage, my wife Tonya and I didn't have any difficulty communicating about money. Why? We didn't have any money to talk about! Having no money gave us a common foundational narrative: "We're flat broke." We also had a common objective: work hard, save, and stop surviving on ramen noodles. We didn't have to talk about these shared understandings because they were obvious.

Our conflicts about money began later in our marriage, after we'd both started our careers and begun to earn more. Having a little money raised questions without obvious answers: How much should we save for the future? Should we merge our bank accounts or keep our money separate? Do we need to ask each other for permission to buy something expensive? Is it wrong to want some financial freedom?

I had expected money to be a source of comfort and security. Instead, having more money highlighted our different opinions and expectations about using and managing our resources.

When our first child, Gavin, arrived, I felt an intense need to provide for my family no matter the sacrifice. I worried constantly about being on the edge of financial disaster, so I dedicated myself to work, hoping to achieve success and earn more. While Tonya acknowledged the importance of financial stability, she also believed that quality time together as a family, fostering our bond, was crucial. However, this perspective only sparked new disagreements on how we should allocate our finances and our time. That's when things got really interesting—it was like trying to balance a checkbook while defusing a bomb. Our disputes shed light on the contrasting ways in which our respective families handled money, resulting in even more conflicts between us.

As our family increased in size, we had several honest conversations about our priorities and aspirations. Through hard work, emotional arguments, and lots of trial and error, we now have a process that works for us.

Today, I wouldn't say Tonya and I *love* talking about our finances. But our money conversations are no longer the heated, stressful fights they once were. We have a deeper understanding of each other's fears, priorities, and goals. We don't need to fight to find common ground. It's not a battle; it's just how we move through life together. To me, that's what marriage is all about.

I have now discovered that there are proven methods for couples to effectively communicate about money and future goals. Looking back, I wish Tonya, and I had known these invaluable lessons when we first got married. Instead, we learned through trial and error, which was not easy. With this book, I hope to save others from going through the same struggles and help them start off on the right path. My goal is to share the hard-earned knowledge I have gained with other couples who may need some guidance in this area. This book will address common fears related to finances in relationships and teach you how to have productive discussions to align your financial goals. In the second half of the book, I will provide practical and adaptable strategies for building a strong financial foundation, to help you pursue your financial goals.

Now, let's get back to Simon and Michelle. Their money problems didn't start in my office—they started a lot earlier than that.

The Disney Dilemma

Michelle's coworker had recently returned from a vacation to Disney World. Over lunch, this coworker showed Michelle tons of pictures of herself, her husband, and their two kids having a ball at the Magic Kingdom.

"We really needed the change of pace," her coworker said. "The kids loved meeting all their favorite characters! And those rides! Those shows! It was the best vacation we've ever been on. We'll never forget it."

Her family sure did look happy in the photos. Michelle couldn't remember the last time her whole family had even been on a vacation. Simon's career was demanding, but from the way he spoke about it, it sounded like he was settling in nicely. Soon, the kids would be teenagers, and they wouldn't be interested in a vacation like Disney World. Time was flying by!

After dinner, when the kids had gone to bed, Michelle brought it up. "You won't believe what I heard today," she said as they put the dishes away. "My friend at work just came back from a Disney World vacation with her kids. The pictures looked amazing. They had so much fun and made so many memories. Don't you think we should do something like that, too?"

"Sounds nice, honey, but you know we can't afford that right now," Simon said. "We've been saving, but Disney's so expensive. We need to be smart with our money. Maybe in a few years."

"We have enough money to pay for a trip," Michelle said. "There are some good deals online right now. We've both been working hard—we deserve a break! Plus, in a few years, the kids won't even want to go. Come on, Simon, let's do this for us."

Simon sighed. "I know you mean well, but you're being unrealistic. We can't spend all our savings on a trip. What if the car breaks down or the roof leaks or one of us gets sick? Plus, I can't just take off time from work. It's too hectic. Now's my chance to prove myself and ensure I keep climbing the ladder."

"Haven't you proven yourself enough?" Michelle asked. "They should let you take a week off, or at least use your vacation days."

Simon shook his head. "I'm managing this new project. It'll take a lot of time and effort, but it'll benefit the team, and they want me to be in charge. If I perform well now, I could get a big promotion in the future. You know this is what I've been working toward. Now's not the right time for a Disney vacation."

Neither Simon nor Michelle was happy with the outcome of that conversation. Both felt like their concerns were obvious, and both felt like those concerns were being shrugged off.

What would be the better choice? Should they go on vacation now, when the kids are young, or wait until they have more money?

It's more complicated than a simple yes-or-no answer. That's why learning how to communicate, and how to get to the root of the conflict, is more important than determining the "right" answer. There is no "right" answer. So, let's break down their concerns.

Simon was thinking about the vacation through the lens of *providing*. He was thrilled about the opportunity to lead a new project at work, which would open the door to a promotion, a higher salary, and the ability to provide for his family in the way he thinks they deserve. He had always dreamed of being a leader and making a difference in his field, and this opportunity was the culmination of all his hard work. If he excelled at this project, he'd be able to provide his family with a more secure financial life. He loves his family more than anything and wants to give them the best life possible!

Meanwhile, Michelle was thinking about the vacation through the lens of *bonding*. She knew Simon had been spending a lot of time working, and his demanding work kept him away from home more often than not. She saw that their financial situation was improving, especially since she herself had gone back to work part-time, and she wanted them to enjoy that increased security as a family. She also recognized that their children were growing fast, and the family had a limited amount of time together during this stage of life. She loves her family more than anything and sees the vacation as an opportunity to strengthen their family bonds!

They have the same foundational beliefs—they love their family—and the same goal—a happy, fulfilling life. However, their ideas of how to achieve their shared goal are very different.

Communicating about money is tough if we don't understand where the other person is coming from. Poor communication can easily escalate into an emotional fight or a lot of resentment. Understanding this situation requires both people to listen to what the other is saying, without jumping to conclusions and without immediately defending their own position. They have to be open-minded and ask: "*Why* does my spouse think this way?"

Based on my own personal experiences and those of my clients, I know that this is easier said than done. It's common to simply react based on our own feelings without truly listening to what our partner has to say and why they feel the way they do. For example, Simon may have been stressed about providing for the family, causing him to push back against taking a vacation. Meanwhile, Michelle may have been worried about missing out on creating memories with their kids, prioritizing that over Simon's pursuit of a promotion. In most relationships, this breakdown in communication leads to both sides digging in further and arguing about their beliefs. This downward spiral rarely ends well.

So, what can we do? Simply telling each person to listen to their partner and try to understand their perspective doesn't always work. We need to dig deeper and understand the underlying reasons for each person's stance. What drives us to take our side of the argument? Why is it such an ingrained belief? What deep-seated fears are influencing our thoughts and actions? Do you know why you react in a certain way? Once we have a deeper understanding of these fears and motivations, it becomes much easier to come to a mutual understanding and not let money or other external factors get in the way of our relationship. Trust me, I've tried telling someone to just listen to the other person, and it's like talking to a brick wall. We need to do the work of truly understanding each other—and ourselves—first, before we can find a solution together.

Being able to talk about money is more important than having money

Another surprising discovery I noticed from clients was that simply being able to discuss money, even if doing so was uncomfortable or awkward, was more crucial than having a financial safety net. I was taken aback to learn that when it comes to common money-related stressors like anxiety, stress, avoidance, and feeling uncared for, having money does not guarantee a better relationship if you cannot openly communicate about it. In fact, avoiding conversations about money can worsen your relationship regardless of how much money you have.

CHAPTER 2

THE VIEW FROM
THE ADVISOR'S CHAIR

Money is a huge part of all our lives, whether we like it or not. It seems like it should be easy to discuss something we use every day. But it can seem like every purchase decision involves stress, guilt, or confusion. Can we afford this? Is there a cheaper alternative? Should we buy online or at a store? Should we go out to eat or cook at home? Should I shop at the grocery store with more choices or at the one that's cheaper? It's a never-ending battle of what-if scenarios on every purchase—and that's just the day-to-day.

A study conducted by Bankrate in March 2024 provides insights into the stress associated with money and making everyday purchases. The study revealed that financial stress is a significant issue for many Americans, with 47% of U.S. adults reporting that money negatively impacts their mental health, including causing stress. Key findings from the study include the following: (3)

- Difficulty paying for everyday expenses was the top-cited money-related issue negatively impacting mental health, with 59% of respondents reporting major impacts.

- Inflation and rising prices were a major concern, with 65% of those who cited the economy as the primary cause of their stress specifically mentioning inflation and rising prices as a factor.

- The rise in consumer goods prices has affected other money-related issues that cause stress, such as not having sufficient emergency savings, being in debt, and not having enough discretionary spending money.

- Low-income households were more likely to report financial stress, with 53% of those earning less than $50,000 expressing concerns about money.

- Women were more likely to experience financial stress than men, with 51% of women and 42% of men reporting negative mental health effects from money.

The study highlights that the stress of making everyday purchases is a significant component of overall financial stress for many Americans. Persistent high prices and inflation have made it increasingly difficult for individuals to afford basic necessities, leading to anxiety and worry about their financial situation.

Our personal finances hold great importance for us, as they require responsible management to ensure our financial stability. Our personal finances are like a high-stakes game of financial Jenga—one wrong move and it all comes toppling down! We strive to make wise decisions with our money, avoiding unnecessary expenses and monetary strain on our lives. It's crucial to maintain a healthy balance between saving and spending, enjoying the present while planning for the future.

Finances go beyond numbers on a spreadsheet; they impact both our current situation and our future. This adds an emotional element to managing money. In a relationship, this can become even more complex as two individuals bring their own beliefs and values about money into the mix. It can be challenging to find a harmonious approach when both partners have different perspectives on how money should be handled. Sometimes, it may seem like managing money together is more difficult than handling it alone. No wonder arguments about money in a relationship don't always come to a happy ending.

A study conducted by Kansas State University, led by Sonya Britt, found that arguments about money are the top predictor of divorce. This research utilized longitudinal data from over 4,500 couples as part of the National Survey of Families and Households. The study revealed that financial arguments are more intense and longer lasting than other types of disputes, significantly decreasing relationship satisfaction and increasing the likelihood of divorce, regardless of income, debt, or net worth levels. (4)

Additionally, a survey by Ramsey Solutions in 2017 supports these findings, indicating that money-related fights are the second leading cause of divorce in the U.S., after infidelity. The survey highlighted that couples with significant debt and poor communication about finances are particularly prone to stress and conflict, which can lead to divorce. (5)

As a financial advisor, I have a unique perspective on how money affects people's lives in different ways. I work with a wide range of clients with varying financial situations and goals. I see the whole spectrum of financial realities, from poor to rich, and

I see how money influences feelings, choices, challenges, and aspirations. I also get to see how couples communicate or don't communicate about money.

Discussing finances with a spouse can be challenging for various reasons, as it often brings up emotional baggage from past experiences and relationships, which can lead to uncomfortable or tense conversations. Fear of being judged or criticized can result in defensiveness or reluctance to open up, further exacerbating the situation. Differences in values and priorities in terms of spending, saving, and financial goals can cause conflicts within the relationship.

During a recent counseling session, a married couple named Dave (48) and Susan (43) discussed the ongoing tension they experienced during financial conversations. Susan explained, "Whenever we talk about money, I walk on eggshells because Dave doesn't trust me. I used to have a problem with shopping. I would make several clothing purchases each day and bring the items home but never wear them. Later in the month, I would return the items or, if I couldn't return them, I would sell them online. Even though I'm better now, every purchase I make gets questioned. We even argue about small things like buying sneakers for our kids."

The couple's approach to money conversations was characterized by an "us against each other" mentality rather than an "us against the problem" attitude. As a result of their communication difficulties, the couple had accumulated debt and were struggling to create a strong vision for their financial future. Past experiences and emotional baggage can significantly impact financial discussions between partners. This highlights the importance of addressing the emotional aspects and childhood background that may contribute to money struggles in relationships.

To overcome Dave and Susan's challenges, we worked on setting rules for financial discussions that were supportive and productive. All financial purchases, assets, and debts would be fully disclosed to achieve transparency, and the focus would be on solving differences and challenges together rather than debating who was right or wrong.

What are we talking about?

Another challenge I see is a lack of financial literacy, and a sense of vulnerability around this topic can make it difficult for both parties to express their true feelings about money matters. Additionally, power dynamics within the relationship can lead to one partner feeling dominated or undermined, while the other may feel they must suppress their own opinions and desires.

Laura and Alex, a couple in their 30s, faced numerous challenges related to financial literacy, vulnerability, and power dynamics in their relationship. Initially, they both possessed similar levels of knowledge and interest in managing their finances. However, over time, Alex took on the responsibility of handling their money while Laura focused on other household tasks. This division created a growing gap in their financial literacy, with Alex becoming more proficient and Laura's skills remaining stagnant. As a result, there was an imbalance in their relationship, where Alex felt more confident and in control while Laura felt increasingly vulnerable and dependent. Due to her lack of knowledge, Laura found it challenging to express her opinions and desires regarding their finances, as she feared that doing so would undermine her position. This created tension between the couple as they struggled to effectively communicate about money. Laura's reluctance stemmed from her emotional baggage of feeling inadequate, while Alex often dismissed Laura's concerns due to feeling burdened with financial responsibilities.

Some effective ways to improve financial literacy in a relationship are to:

- **Be transparent about finances:** Open and honest communication about money matters is crucial. Couples should share information about their income, debts, assets, and financial goals to build trust and avoid financial infidelity.

- **Plan for the future together:** Work on creating joint financial goals and strategies for achieving those goals. This collaborative approach helps both partners understand and contribute to their shared financial future. (7)

Despite the obstacles discussed in this chapter so far, open communication about finances is crucial for the health and longevity of a relationship. Through effective communication, couples can work together to achieve their financial goals and find common ground in their values and priorities. It takes courage to have difficult conversations about money, but the benefits far outweigh the discomfort.

As couples work to overcome these obstacles, it's important to remember that the process of discussing finances can be just as valuable as the outcome. In a lot of ways, communication is more valuable than money! Let me say it again: Being able to discuss money will strengthen your relationship and improve your financial decision-making. (6)

The taboo of talking about money

Growing up, my mother taught me that certain topics were off-limits for discussion with other people: money, sex, religion, and politics. These conversations were considered "rude" or "vulgar." However, issues like health problems and relationship troubles were perfectly acceptable to discuss in public. My mother would talk about money but not really delve into it; she might mention buying a new car or someone getting a new job, but never the specifics of how much was spent or earned.

But just like we seek advice and learn from others about our health and relationships, it's important to do the same about money. Talking about finances is often seen as taboo due to cultural norms and taboos. In many societies, discussing personal wealth and income is considered inappropriate because it can be seen as a comparison of social status. This can lead to feelings of discomfort or even offense. Additionally, talking about money can have social repercussions such as judgment or being ostracized. To avoid potential conflicts, people often choose to keep their financial matters private.

Interestingly, people may feel more comfortable discussing sensitive topics with strangers rather than with friends and family. This could be because strangers are less likely to judge us since they don't have a personal stake in our lives. The anonymity of speaking to someone we don't know also creates a sense of freedom and safety that allows us to open up about sensitive issues without fear of long-term repercussions.

An advantage of speaking with a financial advisor about money is that we can provide independent advice without the emotional baggage that often accompanies discussing money with friends or family. This allows for more open and productive conversations about finances.

Good and bad lessons from our parents

Our parents were the ones who taught us how to manage money, showing us both the right and wrong ways to handle it. The role of our parents in shaping our attitudes and behaviors toward money cannot be underestimated. Whether those habits are good or bad, they have a profound impact on our financial well-being. This phenomenon of intergenerational transfer of financial habits has been extensively studied in psychology and personal finance. Let's take a closer look at the concepts involved:

- **Unconscious learning:** We often learn about money from our parents without even realizing it. Their attitudes, behaviors, and decision-making processes unconsciously shape our own understanding of money.

- **Emotional imprinting:** Our emotional relationship with money is highly influenced by that of our parents. If they were anxious about finances, we may develop similar anxieties.

- **Financial scripts:** Our beliefs about money are often inherited from our parents, whether positive (e.g., "saving is important") or negative (e.g., "money is the root of all evil").

- **Spending and saving patterns:** Our approach to spending and saving is largely influenced by what we observed growing up. If our parents were frugal, we may tend toward frugality ourselves.

- **Risk tolerance:** Our willingness to take financial risks can also be shaped by our parents' approach to financial risk-taking.

- **Financial literacy:** The level of financial education we receive at home can greatly impact our financial literacy as adults.

- **Money taboos:** If money was a taboo subject in our childhood home, we may struggle to discuss finances openly as adults.

- **Generational patterns:** Financial habits can be passed down through multiple generations, creating long-standing familial financial patterns.

- **Overcompensation:** In some cases, people develop habits that are the opposite of those of their parents as a response to perceived financial mistakes.

- **Socioeconomic influence:** Our parents' financial situation during our childhood can shape our perceptions of what is considered normal financially.

It's crucial to understand that while our parents' influence is significant, it does not determine our financial future. As adults, we have the power to examine these inherited habits, keep the beneficial ones, and work on changing those that do not serve us well. By educating ourselves and being self-aware, we can break negative cycles and establish healthier financial habits, even if they were not modeled for us growing up. (8)

When I was growing up, my parents hardly ever talked about money in front of me. When they did, it was usually negative. Conversations were about the fridge breaking and how much it would cost to fix it. Or how the electric bill was too high and we had to stop using the toaster. Or how the neighbor's dog ate the lottery ticket, which had been sure to be a winner this time. These conversations led me to believe money was a source of stress and anxiety, and that there was never enough of it. Those beliefs shaped my relationship with money as an adult.

The Family dinner

When I was young, my family rarely dined out, and when we did, it was usually on special occasions only. I still remember the vibrant lights and colors of the bustling restaurant welcoming us as we walked in. I see the cozy booths, the busy waitstaff, and the inviting menu. There was one golden rule when we ate out: We could only order from the left side of the menu. "The right side of the menu is for rich people, not for us," said my father. On one occasion, we somehow ended up at a nicer restaurant, either for a graduation or a death—or, more likely, because we'd taken a wrong turn. My eyes drifted to the right side of the menu. The restaurant had lobster. Feeling brave, I asked my dad, "Is lobster good? Can we try it?"

My father looked at me with pity. "Son, you don't want to eat lobster. A lobster is a hard-shelled crustacean that lives on the seafloor, scavenging the dead stuff that sinks to the bottom. It's like eating a giant underwater cockroach."

Boy, that sure sounded gross to me! Plus, Dad had spoken with such authority—he knew what he was talking about. Why would anyone want to eat a giant cockroach? I went back to the left side of the menu and ended up with chicken pasta.

Years later, when I was in my 20s, I was out to dinner with friends. "Let's try the lobster here," a friend of mine suggested. "I've heard it's great."

"Lobster?! Why?" My outburst got the attention of the table.

I launched into a lecture about lobsters, cockroaches, and scavenging. When I was finally finished, my friend stared at me and said, "Where'd you get all that from? Lobster's delicious!" He ordered it, I tried it, and of course it was a pure buttery marvel. I'd never tasted anything so good.

The next time I saw my father, I told him about my discovery—that he'd been wrong about lobster the whole time. Dad laughed. "What are you talking about? Me and your mom love lobster!"

"Wait, what? But what about that story you told me? And all the reasons to not eat lobster?"

"That's all factually true," Dad said. "I didn't want to lie to you. But you were only 12, and I wasn't buying you lobster no matter how good they are!"

Fathers! My father's money-saving belief had become my own belief, and I'd never questioned it—not until a trusted friend had an opportunity to challenge it.

As adults, we've all figured out how to deal with money on our own. We probably lacked instruction and didn't have anyone to listen to our woes. We picked up some bad habits and beliefs from our family tree. Then, we fell in love with someone who's just as clueless and messed up as we are! It's no wonder talking about money can be so challenging.

CHAPTER 3

FINANCIAL FEARS

B esides the stress money inevitably brings into our lives and the challenges we face when discussing it—not only with our spouses but also with friends and family—there's an intricate web of factors contributing to our communication struggles. Beyond the lessons we've absorbed from our parents (both positive and negative), there lies a deep-seated fear—a fear that might be conscious or hidden, but that significantly influences how we handle our finances.

It's a fear that has its roots in our very survival. From the earliest days of humanity, the acquisition and management of resources was a matter of life and death. In ancient times, food, shelter, and protection were all dependent on one's ability to gather and protect resources. And in today's world, where money has become the means to acquire those resources, our fear of not having enough is deeply ingrained in our psyche.

In essence, money conversations are like navigating a complex maze, with emotions, upbringing, and fears all playing a role. And just like in a maze, it's easy to get lost, to hit dead ends, and to feel helpless and overwhelmed. But with patience, understanding, and a willingness to confront our fears, we can find our way through and come out stronger on the other side. However, we all have fears and worries that our partner may not fully understand, and we often try to use money as a way to ease those concerns. Unfortunately, this can sometimes backfire and end up amplifying our partner's fears instead.

Let's get back to our friends Simon and Michelle, who are at an impasse with their Disney vacation. We know they have the same beliefs (loving their family is important) and the same goal (to have a fulfilling life). However, Simon is putting work ahead of spending time with the family, while Michelle is prioritizing spending time together over Simon's long hours. So, what's driving them apart?

Let's imagine Simon and Michelle were never able to have an honest conversation about their financial fears. How might that have played out in their lives?

Simon, an engineer for a NASCAR team, loved his family, but he also loved his career, which required him to travel to many races across the country and work long hours at the shop designing the next race car. He was proud of his achievements, enjoyed the recognition and rewards, and brought in a high and stable income for his family.

However, Simon's busy schedule also meant he missed many of his sons' baseball games. The games were important to the kids and Michelle alike. After Simon rejected Michelle's proposal for a Disney vacation, their fights escalated. As Simon missed more games for work, Michelle accused Simon of neglecting the family. Simon defended his work ethic and his responsibility for their lifestyle. They both regretted Simon being less involved in their sons' lives, but they enjoyed the high income and bonuses. They had a beautiful home and could afford to travel for their kids' baseball games from middle to high school.

Though they didn't go on any long vacations, like Michelle's dream Disney trip, they did go on an annual beach weekend. However, even on those trips, Simon seemed distracted by work. He could never fully relax and enjoy himself. Sometimes, he spent vacation days faxing designs back and forth to the office. Michelle felt resentful and frustrated that Simon couldn't leave his work behind. She wondered if he loved her or the family at all. If he did, why did he seem so reluctant to spend time with them? She wondered if her sons would be affected by Simon's absence. She wished Simon would realize what he was missing and prioritize his family more.

Michelle urged Simon to reconsider his work habits and set better boundaries with his boss and colleagues. She was ready to change their lifestyle if he was ready to change his job or reduce his hours. She suggested they downsize their home, vacation differently, and drop other luxuries if that would allow him to spend more time with her and their sons. Simon didn't believe that downsizing was possible with all their expenses, such as mortgage, bills, the kids' activities, retirement savings, and college tuition. He felt that Michelle did not fully understand how expensive their lifestyle was and would continue to be into retirement. He felt it was impossible to reduce the momentum of his career. He saw no other option but to keep working at the same level.

Simon and Michelle were never able to come to a satisfying compromise for them both. Simon kept working long, hard hours to bring in his high income, and Michelle continued to feel isolated and neglected. Simon was exhausted and burned out from work.

After the boys went to college, Simon and Michelle filed for divorce.

So, what happened? Why were they not able to come to a compromise?

This terrible outcome for their marriage can be traced directly to Simon and Michelle's *fears* about money, which were similarly present in their argument about the Disney vacation, albeit on a smaller scale.

Simon thought about their Disney vacation, and their life, through the lens of *providing*. The flip side of that is the fear that, somehow, he would be *unable* to provide and the family would fall into financial catastrophe. As he ascended the career ladder, he couldn't shake the feeling that a few missteps could jeopardize his job security. Whether this perception was accurate or not, the fear weighed heavily on him. For Simon, providing financial stability for his family became an expression of love. If he couldn't ensure that security, he felt like a failure. This fear gripped him so tightly that the idea of working less seemed impossible. Understanding the effects of financial stress, a heavy workload, and the pressure to provide that is often associated with the current cultural understanding of manhood can be important in supporting men through this stressor. (9)

Michelle thought about their vacation, and their life, through the lens of *bonding*. Her fear was *disconnection*. For Michelle, the emotional security she felt with her husband and sons was just as important, or even more important, than the financial security. It's not that she wasn't concerned about finances, but that she was equally concerned with their relationship. When Simon chose work over time with his family, Michelle feared that the emotional foundation of their family was weakening.

In the end, Michelle and Simon were never able to communicate effectively about their fears, and thus were never able to come to a solution that made them both happy. Michelle was never able to build the deep connection with Simon she needed, and Simon was only able to reduce his work hours when there was no longer a family to support. As a result, even though they both loved their family and wanted a fulfilling life, their financial fears became self-fulfilling prophecies.

Many of our arguments and hurt feelings in marriage stem from not understanding that the other person is trying to avoid a different type of conflict or fear.

Men's fears and financial stress

Many married men share the fear of losing their job or being unable to provide for their family, regardless of whether this fear is rational or not. It's this fear itself that causes concern, not the actual reality. It's a heavy, persistent fear that clings like a shadow to even the most financially secure, driving them to toil endlessly in the pursuit of stability. Of course, losing a job is a possibility for anyone as a result of company downsizing, economic downturns, losing major clients, or other factors beyond our control. The thought of losing our source of income drives us to work harder and longer, believing that if we just save enough money and build a bigger financial cushion, everything will be better. But even when we think we have enough saved up, the stress never seems to go away. From my perspective as an advisor, it doesn't matter how much money someone has; in their eyes, it's never enough.

I recently worked with a client who had been a high-ranking executive at the same company for 26 years and was considering retiring within the next four years. Despite his long tenure and financial stability, he still feared losing his job. However, I reassured him that even if he were to lose his job tomorrow, he would be financially secure. There was no need for him to continue working for an additional three years out of fear of losing his job, and he should only do so to achieve his personal goal of working for the company for 30 years.

I have several clients who are in the early stages of their careers, or halfway through, and they all share the same fear: losing their job. And for them, this fear may be more warranted than for others. What's intriguing is that both those embarking on a new career and those reaching the end of their career experience the same level of anxiety.

I have a client who started his own business several years ago and achieved great success. Two years ago, he sold the company for a substantial amount. As he was a long-standing client, I recently met with him and his wife to ask how retirement was treating them. However, instead of receiving happy responses, his wife appeared unhappy. She mentioned that they initially enjoyed traveling and spending time with their grandchildren, but now her husband was already looking for another business to start or purchase. He expressed discomfort with their savings and felt the need to continue working.

A report in 'the *Journal of Occupational Health Psychology* on "Psychological Well-Being in Retirement" highlights the issue of self-perception and identity, with many men strongly identifying with their work roles. It shows that previous work roles continue to shape retirees' identities even after retirement. This attachment to work identity can make it difficult for some men to transition into retirement, regardless of their financial situation. In addition, studies show that men's psychological well-being in retirement is more strongly influenced by financial, social, and job resources compared to women. This suggests that men may place a higher value on their ability to continue earning, even when it's not strictly necessary. (10)

While Simon and Michelle's story is fictional, as an advisor I consistently encounter a significant issue with clients: the tension between work demands and quality of life. Occasionally, couples manage to find a compromise, but unfortunately, it's all too common for marriages to falter—even when both partners deeply desire a different outcome.

I'd like to emphasize that it's not exclusively men who sometimes prioritize work excessively, focusing on providing for the family while inadvertently neglecting family time. This role can also be assumed by women, with men taking on a more nurturing position. Additionally, I've encountered couples where both partners are hyper-focused on financial security, as well as couples who adopt a more carefree approach to work, prioritizing family well-being above all else. What's important to recognize is the type of person you are and the type of person your partner is. By understanding your differences, you can better understand how to communicate with each other and what lies behind your partner's decision-making.

Women's fears and financial stress

In many marriages, women are often the leaders of the household. They make daily decisions about managing the household, taking care of children, and other family needs. In this role, women also take on the responsibility of nurturing relationships and building a sense of community, including within their marriage.

An article titled "The science behind financial stress and the gender divide" (11) reveals that women's fears often revolve around the strength and stability of their relationship with their husband. They may fear losing emotional security or experiencing isolation and disconnection in their marriage. Balancing career growth and family responsibilities is a common concern for women, as this can affect their earning potential and financial stability. Many women have fears about becoming financially dependent on their partner or being unable to support themselves if the relationship ends.

Women also tend to worry more about long-term financial security, especially in retirement, due to their longer life expectancy. This means they may need to plan for more years of financial support. With career breaks often taken for caregiving, women's lifetime earnings and retirement savings can also be impacted. Debt is another source of stress for both genders, but women tend to express more anxiety about managing and paying off debts such as student loans, credit card debt, and mortgages.

Women may feel less confident in making financial decisions, leading to increased stress and worries about money matters. Additionally, women are more likely to take on caregiving responsibilities for children or elderly parents, which can come with associated costs and potential impacts on their careers and finances. (11)

Women can also feel higher levels of anxiety and depression compared to men. According to a Bankrate poll, 46% of women say money issues negatively affect their mental health, compared to 38% of men. This includes feelings of anxiety, depression, sleeplessness, and stress. (12)

Greater concern over daily financial management

Women are more concerned than men about having enough emergency savings and being able to pay for everyday expenses. This heightened concern over daily financial management can lead to more frequent and intense stress responses. For instance, 60% of women worry about emergency savings compared to 53% of men, while 59% of women are stressed about paying for everyday expenses versus 53% of men. (12)

Emotional responses to financial situations

Women are more likely to experience negative emotions in response to financial situations. For example, checking a bank account or facing unexpected expenses triggers more negative emotions in women than in men. About 52% of women feel negative emotions when checking their bank account compared to 46% of men, and 73% of women feel stressed by unexpected expenses versus 64% of men. (12)

Broader societal and economic factors

Women's financial stress is also influenced by broader societal and economic factors, such as long-standing pay disparities and cultural expectations around gender roles in financial management. These systemic issues can compound personal financial stress and its impact on mental health. (12)

Financial stress affects women's mental health more severely than men's due to higher levels of anxiety and depression, greater concern over daily financial management, significant impacts on sleep and physical health, more intense emotional responses to financial situations, long-term financial vulnerability, lower financial confidence, and broader societal and economic factors.

Trusted loved ones

Open communication about financial concerns with trusted loved ones can provide emotional relief and support for women dealing with financial stress. This support system can offer a safe space to share fears and worries, gain new perspectives, and potentially find solutions.

Many women tend to keep their financial concerns to themselves, fearing judgment or feeling embarrassed about their situation. However, opening up and discussing their challenges and anxieties can bring a sense of relief and validation. Trusted loved ones, such as close friends or family members, can offer empathy, understanding, and practical advice. Sharing financial worries with others may also lead to new perspectives or ideas that could help improve the situation. Loved ones may have insightful suggestions based on their own experiences or knowledge that the individual may not have considered before. Moreover, when someone shares their financial struggles with others, it often creates a ripple effect of openness where others feel more comfortable sharing their own money concerns. This can create a supportive community where individuals feel less alone in their struggles. Finally, in addition to providing emotional support, opening up about financial problems can lead to practical solutions. For example, family members may be able to offer advice on budgeting and saving strategies.

However, it's essential to choose who you share your financial concerns with carefully. It's best to confide in someone you trust and who will respect your privacy. It's also important to consider if the person you are confiding in is knowledgeable about personal finance matters and can offer helpful advice. In some cases, seeking professional help from a financial advisor or therapist may also be beneficial for managing stress related to money matters.

Talking about our fears

How do we go about having open and honest discussions with our partner regarding our underlying fears and worries about money? It can be tough to bring up these deep-seated beliefs, as they often remain hidden, making it hard to talk about them with our significant other. The main issue lies in understanding our partner's emotions surrounding finances. When faced with financial stress, our immediate reactions may unintentionally push our partner to their limits.

For example, if your spouse suggests a dinner date, you might worry about the cost. Suggesting a more budget-friendly alternative, like enjoying premade dinners from Costco, could be misinterpreted as disinterest in spending quality time together. Without grasping the reasons behind each other's reactions, true understanding is lacking.

However, if we can comprehend each other's perspectives, there's another solution: How about grabbing some stuffed peppers and a bottle of wine from Costco for a cozy backyard picnic for just the two of us? Win–win.

Of course, you have to understand that Costco won't always be the right option—even though I love Costco, sometimes you have to spend the money on a nice date night out.

CHAPTER 4

HOW TO COMMUNICATE

S o, now that we understand possible fears and how those fears shape our decision-making, how do we constructively talk to our partner about them?

Is there any logic to this?

First, it's important to know yourself, identify your own fears, and examine how realistic they are. Ask yourself how they are affecting your ability to love your partner. How likely is it that you'll lose your job if you don't work late every night? How likely is it that your kids will resent you if you postpone one vacation? You have to find a balance between your own fears and your partner's fears.

Finances shape our lives in many ways, and our finances are much more than numbers in an Excel spreadsheet. When we acknowledge that financial decisions are rooted in emotion, it becomes much easier to talk about them. It's important to recognize that while our partner's fears may seem illogical or hard to understand, they are very real! When our partner expresses financial fears, we need to take those fears seriously and treat them with respect.

Approach the conversation with curiosity

There is no single "right way" to manage your finances. The best way is the way that works best for you. You don't need to come into these conversations with guns blazing and a plan to "fix" everything.

Unfortunately, financial conversations are not one-and-done. As your relationship, family, and careers develop, so will your financial needs and goals. So, it's best to communicate regularly with your partner about your financial lives. I recommend scheduling regular "check-in" conversations about finances. When I'm beginning an advisement relationship with my clients, I recommend we meet once every few weeks until we're all on the same page. Then, we meet every three months, and eventually twice a year. A similar schedule may work in your relationship. Start by scheduling check-ins every few weeks, and then gradually decrease the frequency as your habits and patterns become established. The most important thing is to have open conversations about money on a regular basis.

Do we really have to talk about this?

Avoiding discussions about money can exacerbate financial stress. Research from Cornell University indicates that individuals under financial stress are less likely to discuss their concerns with their partners, leading to a vicious cycle where stress and avoidance feed into each other. (13)

Lack of communication about finances can deteriorate the quality of a relationship. Couples who avoid financial discussions may experience financial infidelity, where one partner hides financial information to avoid conflict. Over time, this lack of transparency and communication can erode trust and intimacy in the relationship. (13) Meanwhile, couples who view financial issues as unsolvable are more likely to avoid discussing them. This perception can lead to perpetual conflicts, as unresolved financial issues continue to resurface, creating ongoing tension and dissatisfaction. (13)

It is not necessary to share the same values as your partner, but it is important to understand and respect their values. Doing so can greatly improve your relationship.

Let go of black-and-white thinking

When we're driven by fears, it's easy to be resistant to any kind of change. But there's good news! Now that we understand the dynamics and how deeply hidden they are inside of us, we can break the vicious cycle of triggering fears. Be patient with each other, talk more about your fears, and think about how you can support each other. Tell your spouse how they can help you, what you need, and what you can do to help them. The beauty of how God created us is that, yes, we have different fears and needs, and yes, it's easy to get into arguments, but this also creates an opportunity for closeness and intimacy.

Let's think about Simon and Michelle again. How could their Disney vacation dilemma have gone differently?

If Simon and Michelle had spoken honestly about their fears, the conversation may have gone something like this: "Simon, it's important to me that we spend time together as a family. What's going on at work that makes it feel impossible for you to take time off?"

Then, instead of Simon saying it's not the right time, he could continue the conversation with curiosity and openness. He might say, "I'm not comfortable taking a week off work right now, but what is it about your coworker's vacation that excites you? Maybe we can find something local to do now and talk about a longer vacation in the future."

Instead of shutting each other down, they could have opened up the conversation to ask about what fears and desires are being activated. In this way, they would have been able to get out of the black-and-white thinking (we go, or we don't go) and instead think creatively about different solutions to strengthen their relationship.

If Simon and Michelle had practiced these kinds of conversations, when Michelle raised the idea of changing their lifestyle, Simon might have been more amenable to it. They could have worked together instead of falling victim to their fears and eventually ending their marriage. For example, they could have decided to downsize their house and reduce their expenses. Then, as Simon advanced in his career, he could have helped develop a younger engineer on a similar track. Then, Simon would have been able to delegate some of the travel that took him away from home to this younger engineer, eager to develop his career as Simon had been. Perhaps Simon would not have earned the same bonuses from this approach, but instead, he would have gained more time off to spend with his family, thus strengthening the bonds as Michelle needed.

These kinds of decisions and lifestyle changes take a lot of open communication and honest compromise. They're not one-and-done decisions, which is why it's important to have continuing conversations about financial decisions as your life together grows and changes.

Starting a conversation

Starting a dialogue about financial stress with a loved one or partner may seem intimidating, but it's vital for nurturing healthy relationships and financial well-being. Here are steps to guide you in initiating this significant discussion:

- Choose an appropriate time and place: Select a tranquil, private moment when both of you are at ease and have ample time to converse without disruptions.

- Be transparent and honest: Share your specific financial worries openly, expressing how they affect you emotionally. Use "I" statements to focus on your feelings rather than pointing fingers.

- Listen without judgment: Allow your partner room to share their fears and concerns about money without interruptions or defensiveness.

- Focus on common goals: Discuss shared financial aspirations and values to find common ground.

- Avoid criticism: Instead of dwelling on past financial errors, concentrate on constructive ways forward.

- Be specific about your concerns: Clearly outline which aspects of your finances are causing you stress or anxiety.

- Brainstorm solutions together: Collaborate on potential strategies to address financial worries as a team.

- Consider seeking professional help: If needed, involve a financial advisor or counselor for professional guidance.

- Make it an ongoing conversation: Commit to regularly discussing money matters and concerns.

- Express appreciation: Acknowledge your partner's efforts and thank them for engaging in challenging financial discussions.

Approaching money conversations with openness, empathy, and a problem-solving attitude can help you tackle financial fears together and build a solid financial future as partners or a family.

CHAPTER 5

HOW OUR IMPULSIVE RESPONSES BLIND US TO REALITY

In my work with clients and through personal experience, I have noticed a recurring issue: overreactive responses to financial matters that interfere with a relationship. These reactions often stem from our past beliefs or misconceptions about our partner. While not universal, some individuals react disproportionately, to say the least, to situations that seem trivial to their partner and advisor.

When I dig deeper into these reactions, I find that they can often be traced back to our upbringing. Whether we grew up in poverty or in privilege, our financial experiences shape our attitudes and responses toward money and relationships—and sometimes cause us to overreact or believe something that isn't true.

Our internal beliefs?

Just like many other beliefs we hold about the world, our understanding of money is often shaped by the people and circumstances we were exposed to while growing up. The way our parents or caregivers talked about and acted around money, and the consequences we witnessed, all contribute to our perception of its abundance or scarcity, its significance, and its purpose.

Some of us may have adopted similar attitudes toward money as our parents, while others may have consciously chosen to do the opposite to avoid similar outcomes. We tend to firmly believe that our own views on money are correct, making it difficult for us to comprehend how others can have such different perspectives on it.

Whether money was openly discussed at the kitchen table or was a source of arguments, these early experiences form the foundation of our financial mindset.

Common money beliefs and mindsets

Money as a measure of a person's worthiness

For many individuals, money is closely tied to their sense of self-worth and how they view the worth of others. In our society, there is a strong association between financial success and personal value, leading to the belief that having more money equates to being more successful or respected in life.

When someone's net worth is seen as a representation of their overall worth as a person, it can lead to constant comparisons with others. We may feel inadequate if we earn less than a friend or family member, but superior if we know we earn more. This mindset can also cause us to judge our own lives or the lives of others based on financial status, resulting in shame or feelings of failure if our financial situation is not ideal. Ultimately, we all want to feel worthy, and this belief can drive us to strive for wealth or worry about our financial future.

According to an article titled "The Psychology of Money: Unraveling Money Beliefs and Mindset" (14), to address the idea that money determines our worth, it's important to recognize that our value as human beings does not originate from our financial status. There are admirable individuals who have wealth and those who do not, just as there are less admirable individuals who lack wealth and those who have it. Therefore, wealth cannot be relied upon as an indicator of a person's character or worth.

While having a lot of money may come from luck, privilege, hard work, or intelligence, these qualities alone do not define a person's worth. By redefining success for ourselves and focusing on values, personal growth, relationships, and fulfillment rather than the numbers in our bank account or on our paycheck, we can shift away from equating material possessions with self-worth. (14)

The scarcity mindset

The "scarcity mindset" is a term used to describe the belief that there will never be enough money to meet one's needs, or that at some point, one will run out of money and be unable to acquire more. This mindset often stems from childhood experiences with limited resources, witnessing parents lose significant amounts of money, or experiencing financial hardships in adulthood.

A scarcity mindset is a psychological state characterized by the perception that resources, particularly money, are limited and insufficient. This mindset can significantly impact one's financial behaviors and overall well-being. Below are the key aspects of a scarcity mindset and fear of financial insecurity.

A scarcity mindset manifests as a constant focus on what one lacks rather than what one has. It's characterized by feelings of not having enough money to live the life one wants, leading to persistent financial anxiety. (15)

Those with a scarcity mindset may feel constant anxiety and excessive worry about money, leading them to avoid taking financial risks and to focus on buying only the cheapest items regardless of quality. It may also cause overworking, hoarding, or being overly frugal in an attempt to feel in control and safe, even when it may not be necessary.

To overcome this mindset, it's important to evaluate the present situation and determine if past experiences are influencing current beliefs. If there are legitimate reasons for concern, such as low income or a large upcoming expense, it may not be indicative of a scarcity mindset but rather a responsible approach. Seeking advice from someone who appears financially stable can also help provide perspective.

If worries about money stem more from past experiences than from current circumstances, take time to assess the current situation objectively. Ask yourself: How has your life changed since you last faced financial struggles? Have your problem-solving skills and earning potential improved? Who do you have for support now? What community resources are available? What safety nets have you already established? Is the amount of thought and energy you put into preventing financial disaster proportional to the likelihood of it occurring? How much trust do you have in yourself (and your partner, if applicable) to handle financial challenges?

Often, those with financial insecurity forget that they are no longer alone in navigating their finances and fail to recognize their own growth and capabilities since facing similar stressors in the past. Reflecting on past challenges and how you overcame them can also boost your confidence in handling future financial obstacles. Finally, educating yourself on financial planning and taking steps to build a secure future can alleviate some of the fear and anxiety surrounding money.

Other common money mindsets

- Abundance mindset: In contrast to a scarcity mindset, an abundance mindset focuses on opportunities and possibilities. People with this mindset tend to believe there are enough resources for everyone. (16)

- Break-even mindset: This mindset is focused on just making ends meet. People with this mindset often live paycheck to paycheck, with their income closely matching their expenses. (17)

- Rich mindset: People with a rich mindset focus on adding value, leveraging resources, and growing wealth. They often see opportunities where others see obstacles. (17)

- In-debt mindset: This mindset is characterized by a cycle of borrowing and spending. People with this mindset often find themselves in perpetual debt. (17)

- "All-or-nothing" mindset: This mindset can hinder financial progress by discounting smaller amounts of money or efforts as not being enough. (18)

- Risk-averse mindset: People with this mindset tend to avoid financial risks, which can limit their potential for growth and wealth accumulation. (18)

- "Keeping up with the Joneses" mindset: This mindset drives people to spend money to maintain a certain lifestyle or appearance, often at the expense of their financial health. (18)

- Procrastination mindset: This mindset leads to putting off important financial decisions or actions, and potentially missing opportunities or exacerbating financial issues. (16)

- Money avoidance mindset: Some people associate money with negative qualities and may subconsciously avoid dealing with financial matters. (16)

- Money worship mindset: This mindset involves the belief that money is the key to happiness and can solve all problems. (16)

Understanding these various mindsets can help individuals identify their own attitudes to money and potentially shift toward more productive financial behaviors. It's important to note that these mindsets are not fixed and can be changed with awareness, education, and conscious effort.

Overspending

I was advising a couple where the wife became infuriated when her husband spent money on frivolous items. She was a strict saver, having grown up in poverty, and scrutinized every penny. His carefree spending habits drove her mad.

However, in an interesting twist, she had been referred to me by her brother, whom I knew very well. He, too, had grown up in the same financial circumstances and environment. Yet he didn't stress over money and wasn't a big saver. In fact, I would say he was more of a spender than a saver. So, how could siblings raised in the same environment end up with such divergent approaches to finances?

The answer lies in the intricate interplay of individual temperament, learned behaviors, and personal choices. While a shared upbringing provides a common foundation, each sibling develops their unique money mindset based on their distinct personality, experiences, and coping mechanisms.

So, why is one sibling a saver while the other is not? It's a fascinating puzzle—one that underscores the complexity of human behavior and the multifaceted relationship between money and emotions. Regardless, understanding these differences can lead to more compassionate conversations about money within relationships.

We all fall into this trap to some extent. Sometimes, our unwavering convictions are rooted in thoughts that, upon closer examination, turn out to be blatantly incorrect. Yet each of us remains steadfastly convinced that our perspective is undeniably correct.

Your expectations about how others manage money

The origins of our expectations remain mysterious. Regardless of their source, one undeniable truth persists: We wholeheartedly believe in their correctness, and they become etched into the very fabric of our souls. Let's look at a few I frequently see that cause stress in a relationship.

To spend or not spend

Tonya's background: Saving every cent
Growing up, my wife Tonya learned the value of stretching a dollar from her hardworking but financially struggling parents. She saved every penny and counted them like an experienced accountant, always preparing for unexpected expenses. The thought of overspending caused her great anxiety.

My journey: From scarcity to seeking more
I also grew up with hand-me-downs and shared meals like Tonya, but my aspirations went beyond just survival. I wanted to spoil Tonya with things she wouldn't buy for herself, surprising her with special treats from time to time.

Generosity meets resistance
As our love deepened, my desire to pamper Tonya only grew stronger. But she, the self-appointed protector of our finances, resisted every extravagant suggestion I made. Her fear of wasting money and not finding the best deal consumed her.

The battle in silence
I struggled with my own emotions as well. It pained me to see Tonya disappointed whenever I couldn't fulfill my spontaneous ideas. I felt like a clumsy dancer who kept stepping on her toes.

One night, I finally brought up the topic. We sat together on our old couch, holding hands, and I shared my dreams—the ones that required spending rather than just saving. Tonya listened intently and opened up about her fears and her memories of scarcity and guilt surrounding spending money.

The solution
Over time, we both came to understand that our attitudes toward money were shaped by our past experiences. Tonya's frugality

was a way of showing love in tough times, while my generosity was an expression of my love for her. Together, we vowed to honor both sides of our shared history—being smart with money while indulging in life's little luxuries

The fear of debt

In a counseling session, I encountered a couple where the wife ardently emphasized the critical importance of debt elimination. To her, it was the pinnacle of financial well-being—a goal that should tower above all others. She envisioned a life unencumbered by loans, where every dollar earned would be free from interest's grasp.

Her husband, however, harbored a more pragmatic view. While not opposed to the idea, he regarded debt as a necessary companion—a tool to be wielded judiciously throughout life. His heart didn't beat in sync with his wife's fervor, but he was willing to tread the path she advocated. For him, debt wasn't a dragon to slay; it was a partner in their financial journey.

Their differing stances underscored a universal truth: Not everyone perceives debt in the same light. Some see it as a foe to conquer, while others view it as a pragmatic ally. The key is not to decide whose approach is right or wrong but to understand each other's perspectives and find a happy middle ground.

To plan or not to plan

Another reaction I see is around the need to do financial planning or the desire not to do financial planning.

One partner may be the careful planner, someone whose life is meticulously organized, and that's precisely how they prefer it. The same principle applies to their financial outlook—they want to track every dollar coming in and going out, diligently saving for the future. The other partner might take a more laid-back approach. It's quite common for opposites to attract, leading both types to end up in my office. For instance, a gentleman once shared that his parents meticulously planned their financial future, saving every dime and forgoing vacations. Their retirement was meant to be their time to travel and truly enjoy life. Sadly, his father passed away at age 66, and his parents never got to savor those moments. Now, he and his partner focus on maxing out their 401k plans, but that's about all the planning they do. Instead, they strike a balance between planning for the future and enjoying life along the way.

Recognizing our partner's viewpoint

Understanding our own expectations and acknowledging our partner's differing viewpoints is crucial. Both sets of expectations can be valid, even if they are opposite. Often, each person firmly believes their perspective is the only correct one. However, it's essential to recognize that overreacting to our partner's divergent financial expectations can strain the relationship. Balancing understanding and compromise are key to maintaining a healthy partnership.

Maintaining perspective in relationships

Strengthening relationships by talking about money

In any long-term relationship, it's important to take a step back and consider the bigger picture. When conflicts arise, particularly regarding money, it may be easy to assume that our partners do not care for or appreciate us. However, this is not always the case.

We must remind ourselves of the positive aspects of our relationship: the ways in which our spouse supports us and contributes to making it work.

Even when we disagree, trust and love remain at the core. Focusing on building a strong partnership helps us navigate through challenges. Here are some additional insights:

- Open communication: Instead of avoiding discussions about finances, address them directly. Be open and honest about financial matters. Avoiding problems will only make them worse.

- Building bridges: Often, we see ourselves and our partner as separate entities when it comes to money. We build bridges between us only when necessary and then burn them once again. But it doesn't have to be this way. Regular communication can serve as a sturdy bridge connecting our two "islands."

- Understanding different perspectives: Take a step back and try to understand your partner's point of view. Consider their background, beliefs, and insecurities related to money. By actively listening, you can gain insight into their behavior and reactions.

- Teamwork approach: Shift from seeing each other as adversaries to being teammates. When both parties work together toward a common goal, there is no longer a need for conflict. This unity strengthens the relationship.

No turning back

Once you adopt this approach, you may wonder why you ever tried to handle financial matters separately before. The effort you put into understanding each other will be well worth it in the end. Remember, trust and understanding are essential components of a lasting relationship.

Recognizing that trust can be difficult, especially when dealing with finances, is crucial. However, taking the first step—initiating conversations about money—can open up a whole new dynamic in your relationship. As you delve deeper into financial matters, you will gain valuable insights into your partner's thought processes. You will begin to understand why they have certain beliefs about money and where those beliefs come from. These shared discussions pave the way for a closer, more connected relationship.

Assuming positive intentions in relationships

In any relationship, it's important to approach your partner with a sense of understanding and empathy, especially when there are differences of opinion or behavior. Financial matters can be particularly sensitive as they involve personal values and emotions. Instead of jumping to conclusions or assuming the worst, try to see the situation from your partner's perspective. They may be coming from a place of love and concern, even if their actions do not align with your expectations.

Take note of how your partner consistently shows love and care for you. It could be through small gestures like cooking your favorite meal or offering support during a stressful day. By focusing on the positive aspects of your relationship, you can strengthen your bond and create a more resilient partnership. When disagreements arise about finances, remember that both of you share the same goal: to secure a stable future for yourselves and your family.

During heated moments, communicate openly and honestly about your feelings and concerns. Listen to each other's perspectives and be willing to compromise. Through open communication and mutual respect, you can work together to find a solution that the needs and values of both of you. By approaching your relationship with understanding and positive intentions, you can create a harmonious and supportive environment that allows both of you to grow and thrive together as a couple.

CHAPTER 6

WHAT ARE THE KEYS TO A HAPPY MARRIAGE?

It was a warm summer afternoon when a married couple found themselves driving down a quiet country road, the windows rolled down and the breeze tousling their hair. The tension from their earlier argument still lingered between them like a thick fog, but neither of them was brave enough to break the silence.

As they passed a barnyard filled with mules, goats, and pigs, the husband attempted to lighten the mood with a sarcastic comment. "Are those your relatives?" he asked, gesturing toward the animals.

The wife couldn't help but let out a small chuckle at his joke. "Yep, in-laws," she replied with a sly smile, and they both burst into laughter.

For a moment, the tension melted away and they were able to enjoy the peaceful scenery around them. It was moments like these, filled with playful banter and laughter, that reminded them of why they fell in love in the first place.

As they continued down the road, the husband reached over and took his wife's hand in his, the warmth of her touch calming his nerves. They may have had their disagreements and arguments, but they knew that at the end of the day, they were each other's greatest source of comfort and laughter. And that was something to be cherished. (19)

How do we make this work?

A fulfilling marriage is built on the foundations of connection, understanding, and mutual respect between partners.

While it may be difficult to imagine during the excitement of your engagement and wedding planning, there will undoubtedly be challenges in your marriage. Sharing your life with someone requires effort, regardless of how compatible you may seem. Just as we take care of our physical health through proper nutrition and exercise, there are steps we can take to maintain a healthy marriage.

Marriage is a lifelong commitment that involves navigating both high and low moments as both partners grow and change as individuals. To weather these storms and appreciate the good times, we must have the right tools. A strong marriage fueled by love and respect doesn't happen overnight; it requires consistent effort from both partners.

Whether newlyweds or long-time companions, every marriage goes through its own unique ups and downs. While it may sound cliché, periods of stability and predictability are a natural part of married life. Stressful situations, boredom, and ineffective communication are all normal aspects of married life. As they say, "Marriage takes work." And just like anything else in life, you reap what you sow. However, the work of maintaining a successful marriage is not as mundane as chores like cleaning or taking out the trash. Marriage is a sacred bond between two individuals, and each couple defines success in their own way. There is no one-size-fits-all definition of a successful marriage.

However, happy marriages are built on several key principles that foster connection, understanding, and mutual respect. Here are the essential elements that contribute to a successful and fulfilling partnership.

Communication

Effective communication is crucial for a strong and healthy relationship, as I have stated elsewhere in this book. Couples should not only discuss practical matters like schedules and finances but also share their hopes, dreams, and feelings. This creates a safe environment for open and honest expression, which is essential for maintaining a solid partnership.

In a successful marriage, partners communicate frequently and openly. They talk about daily logistics and responsibilities, but they also delve deeper into personal thoughts and emotions. They don't just make decisions for the household or family; they also discuss their observations and bond over shared interests. This aspect of communication is vital to a happy marriage, because it sets the foundation for other important aspects such as commitment, patience, and trust.

Truly open communication is key to long-term marital happiness. It's important to always be truthful about your feelings, but also to be respectful when addressing sensitive topics. Creating a safe space for difficult emotions is crucial for keeping the lines of communication open. Avoid defensiveness and aggression, as they will only create distance between you and your partner.

Practicing active listening ensures that your partner feels heard and understood. Remember that you are both individuals with unique interests and perspectives—there is more to talk about beyond daily routines and work responsibilities.

Respect and kindness

According to Nurturing Marriage, there are 2 secrets to a happy marriage: respect and kindness. (20)

Respect in marriage

A happy and fulfilling marriage relies on the fundamental elements of respect and kindness. These qualities help to cultivate a nurturing environment where both partners feel valued, understood, and connected. In a successful relationship, respect is the cornerstone that supports all other aspects. This involves recognizing and appreciating each partner's individuality, actively listening to their opinions, and embracing their differences.

It also means treating one another with dignity and avoiding detrimental behaviors like sarcasm, criticism, or name-calling. Open and effective communication is vital in maintaining respect; starting conversations with praise and expressing feelings without blame or accusation can strengthen the bond between partners.

Key aspects of respect include:

- **Listening**: Actively engaging with your spouse's thoughts and feelings.

- **Acceptance**: Valuing each other's differences and personal boundaries.

- **Gentleness**: Using a kind tone and avoiding harsh words, especially during disagreements

Kindness in marriage

Showing kindness involves considerate actions, uplifting language, and an overall demeanor of compassion. It helps to create a loving and empathetic environment, which is crucial for maintaining a strong relationship. Even small gestures like leaving supportive notes or offering acts of assistance can greatly improve marital happiness

Examples of kindness include:

- **Acts of service**: Taking on chores or responsibilities that your partner usually handles.

- **Affectionate gestures**: Small acts like hugs, kisses, or even a smile can strengthen emotional bonds.

- **Positive reinforcement**: Regularly expressing appreciation for your partner's efforts and qualities fosters a culture of gratitude in the relationship. (21)

The Impact of Kindness and Respect

Studies have shown that kindness and respect are vital components of marital happiness. (21) Couples who make an effort to engage in positive interactions and show appreciation for one another tend to have healthier and more resilient relationships. On the other hand, negative behaviors like criticism and contempt can cause dissatisfaction and create emotional distance between partners.

In short, fostering respect and kindness in a marriage requires ongoing commitment and conscious effort. By making these values a priority, couples can build a strong and loving partnership based on mutual understanding and admiration.

Conflict resolution

Conflict in marriage is inevitable due to the blending of different personalities, backgrounds, and expectations. However, how couples handle these conflicts can significantly impact the health and happiness of their relationship. Here are some key insights and strategies for conflict resolution in marriage.

Understanding conflict

- **Inevitable differences**: Conflict arises from differences in personality, background, and expectations. These differences can initially attract partners to each other, but they may become sources of tension over time. (22)

- **Unsolvable problems**: Research by Dr. John Gottman suggests that 69% of problems in relationships are unsolvable, often rooted in fundamental personality traits or long-standing issues. Couples should focus on managing these conflicts rather than trying to eliminate them. (23)

Strategies for conflict resolution

- **Accept and adjust**: Recognize and accept differences between yourself and your partner. Adjusting to these differences is crucial for resolving conflicts and maintaining harmony. (22)

- **Focus on one issue**: During arguments, concentrate on one issue at a time to avoid confusion and ensure productive discussions. (22)

- **Attack the issue, not the person**: Approach conflicts by addressing the problem rather than attacking your partner's character. Avoid using global qualifiers like "always" or "never". (22, 24)

- **Effective communication**: Use "I" statements to express feelings and needs, and avoid "mind-reading" or assuming your partner's thoughts or motives. (24)

- **Stay calm**: Emotional calmness is essential during discussions. Take breaks if necessary to prevent escalation and ensure constructive dialogue. (24)

- **Reconciliation after conflict**: After an argument, it's important to reconcile with your spouse, showing care and checking in on their feelings. (24)

- **Biblical principles**: For those who follow religious teachings, applying the biblical principles of love, forgiveness, and commitment can guide conflict resolution. (24)

Practical tips

- **Avoid character assassination**: Focus on behaviors and circumstances rather than attacking your partner's personality. (22)

- **Repair attempts**: Use humor, apologies, and affirmations to de-escalate conflicts and show understanding. (24)

- **Compromise**: Work toward solutions that represent "our way" rather than "my way" or "your way". (24)

By employing these strategies, couples can navigate conflicts constructively, fostering a stronger and more resilient relationship.

It's worth the effort

Marriage, like any other worthwhile endeavor, requires constant effort and dedication from both parties involved. It is not something that can be achieved once and then forgotten about. Instead, it requires ongoing attention and nurturing in order to thrive.

One of the key elements of a successful marriage is communication. Open and honest communication is essential for understanding each other's needs and concerns, and for resolving conflicts in a constructive manner. Without proper communication, misunderstandings and resentment can easily build up and damage the relationship.

Respect and trust are also crucial in any marriage. Partners must have faith in each other and treat each other with kindness and consideration. Without these foundations, a marriage cannot withstand the challenges that inevitably arise.

Intimacy, both physical and emotional, is another essential component of a happy marriage. Couples must make time for each other and prioritize their physical and emotional connection in order to maintain a strong and fulfilling bond.

Commitment is another key factor in a successful marriage. Both partners must be fully committed to each other and to the relationship in order to weather the ups and downs of married life.

It's also important for couples to appreciate and show gratitude for each other. Small gestures of appreciation can go a long way in strengthening a marriage and keeping both partners feeling loved and valued.

Compromise is another important aspect of a healthy marriage. Learning to find a middle ground and make sacrifices for each other's happiness is crucial for maintaining a harmonious relationship.

Shared activities and interests can also bring couples closer together and provide opportunities for bonding and creating new memories.

Constructive conflict management is also vital for maintaining a healthy marriage. Disagreements are inevitable, but learning to communicate respectfully and find solutions together can prevent conflicts from becoming major roadblocks in the relationship.

Finally, forgiveness is essential in any marriage. Both partners must be willing to forgive and move forward after mistakes or conflicts in order to create a lasting and fulfilling relationship.

By actively working on these aspects of a marriage, couples can build a strong and loving partnership that can last forever.

What's Next?

As we wrap up our guide on how to communicate with your spouse about money, let's emphasize the critical role of communication. It's the cornerstone of any successful financial plan and happiness.

Imagine this: You've transitioned from individual players to a dynamic duo—the Batman and Robin of budgeting (minus the capes). Suddenly, the journey feels less like a solo hike and more like a tandem bike ride.

Now, let's talk about money. Not in hushed tones or cryptic whispers, but openly—with the enthusiasm of kids in a candy store. Conversations about finances become your secret sauce. They unlock the next steps organically:

- **Money management**: You'll tackle the nitty-gritty together. Wrangling those unruly expenses? Taming the credit card beast? It's a tag-team effort, and you're both in the ring.

- **Debt demolition**: Armed with communication superpowers, you'll strategize debt elimination.

- **Budget alchemy**: You'll create a budget that actually works!

- **Retirement quest**: Retirement savings? Think of it as your treasure chest buried on a digital island. X marks the spot, and your partner holds the map. Together, you'll sail toward golden sunsets.

So, my financial adventurers, keep those lines of communication wide open. Share your dreams, your fears, and the occasional spreadsheet. Remember, it's not just about dollars—it's about weaving your love story into every financial decision.

CHAPTER 7

FUNDAMENTALS

In this next chapter, we will delve into the basic principles of personal finance. Developing strong money management skills is crucial for effectively handling one's finances. Here are some of the key principles and practices we will cover:

- **Organizing your finances:** The first step is organizing all of your financial accounts, such as credit cards, bank accounts, loans, and investments. This helps you stay on top of your financial standing and make informed decisions.

- **Tracking your spending**: It's important to understand where your money goes each month. Consider using budgeting tools to categorize expenses and identify areas where you can cut back.

- **Creating a budget:** Take into account your income and spending habits when creating a realistic budget. Make sure it covers all necessary expenses while also allowing for savings and discretionary spending.

- **Spending less than you earn:** This essential rule helps prevent debt and encourages saving. By consistently spending less than you earn, you can build financial stability.

- **Building savings**: Set up an emergency fund for unexpected expenses and regularly contribute to savings accounts to increase financial security over time.

- **Limiting debt:** Only take on necessary debt that can be managed, such as for income-generating assets. Avoid high-interest debt like credit cards or unnecessary loans.

- **Investing wisely**: Even small investments can grow over time. Consider employer-sponsored retirement plans or other investment accounts to build wealth.

- **Planning for the unexpected:** Be prepared for emergencies by having insurance and a financial safety net to handle unexpected events without disrupting your financial plans.

Our Story

When Tonya and I got married in 1997, we decided to merge our checking accounts into one. We used that account for everything: deposits, bills, savings, and spending. We opened a savings account and planned to transfer the leftover money at the end of each month into the savings account. We knew we needed an emergency fund, but we had no real idea how much we should keep in it.

At this point, I'd never met with a financial advisor, and I wasn't yet on my personal career path. I'd read you should have six months of expenses saved, such as mortgage or rent, food, utilities, insurance, and so on. That would provide us with a cushion if we hit an unexpected hardship, like job loss or illness. Tonya and I both agreed this sounded like a good plan. The idea was to pay all our bills, and then whatever was left in the account at the end of the month we would sock into the new savings account until we had an emergency fund. Simple, right?

At the time, Tonya was an emergency room nurse and I worked for a software engineering company. We didn't have kids yet, so our expenses should've been easy to control with money left at the end of the month. But it didn't work out that way at all.

We had our own bill-tracking system. We stacked the bills in the kitchen—not out in the open, but not out of sight, either. When a paycheck was deposited into our checking account, we paid down the stack of bills as far as we could. It never seemed to go down all the way. Then, more bills were added to the pile as we waited for the next paycheck. We were never able to totally wipe out the pile. It was our accordion bill monster, lurking right in the kitchen! We couldn't kill it, and whenever we got close, it'd come right back to life stronger than ever.

I'm sure you can picture our heroic attempts to conquer the bill monster, armed only with a calculator and sheer determination. We would valiantly pay down the bills with each paycheck, only to witness the stack magically replenish itself as if it had a mind of its own. It was like a budgeting horror movie, with the accordion bill monster as the unexpected star, stealing the show with its uncanny ability to evade our attempts at financial freedom.

At the end of each month, we had barely any money left, and sometimes none at all! When we were able to save, we'd end up dipping into the savings to cover an unexpected bill or because the checking account fell too low. There was too much month left at the end of the paycheck.

Why couldn't we save? We weren't extravagant, and we shared the same goal of living prudently to save for our future together in our dream home. I was lucky to marry my wife, who is not only gorgeous and smart but thrifty as hell. She can find a bargain like a detective on a mission. We both grew up in loving environments, but without much money. We both had mothers who would take a half-full gallon of milk, fill it up with water, and give it a good shake.

For a few years, we thought we just didn't make enough money. We figured that once we'd advanced in our careers, we'd be able to save more. But that didn't happen. As the years passed, our paychecks increased, but we still weren't saving.

I felt like our checking account was a black hole that swallowed everything we deposited. Once money was deposited, it was gone forever. We'd check our statements every month, hoping to find some error or fraud, but we never did. We were the ones responsible for the disappearing money.

The mother of all budgets

Our next plan of attack was to create a budget. Not any old budget—this would be an advanced budget. The kind of budget only a software engineer could create. The mother of all budgets! We (and by we, I mean I) announced that we would track every dollar going in and out of the account using an elaborate spreadsheet I'd created. The budget would be how we finally got our spending under control and killed the accordion thing in the kitchen.

At the end of the month, we'd pull up the bank statement and compare our spending to our budget. Each month, the budget showed we were supposed to have money left, and each month, we didn't. So, Tonya and I would look at all our purchases and play the "justify this purchase" game. This is not a fun marriage game. It ranks right up there with "the reason we have no money is your spending" game. Fun times.

We were so stressed and frustrated that we soon gave up on budgeting. So, budgeting didn't help, and looking at our bank statement at the end of the month didn't help either. The bank statement only showed us what we had spent, not how we could spend better.

After realizing we were unable to stick to our budget and had no funds left at the end of each month, we knew we needed assistance. We needed to find a way to get organized and learn how to effectively manage our finances.

Do you, too, feel like there's never any money left at the end of the month?

Where does all the money go?

As I balanced the family checking account, it was clear that our paychecks were being deposited and the bills were being paid on a regular basis. The issue arose when there seemed to be no trace of what should have been leftover funds. It was like watching water leak out of a small hole in a bucket.

I began to closely monitor our accounts and take inventory of all our finances, including checking accounts and credit cards. By reviewing our accounts and tracking our expenses, I hoped to identify our spending patterns and gain a better understanding of where our money was going.

Our expenses included both fixed and variable costs. Fixed expenses like mortgage or rent, utilities, insurance, and debt payments were unlikely to change month to month. However, we had more flexibility with variable expenses such as food, clothing, and travel.

To help track expenses, I used spreadsheets that allowed for customization and did most of the calculations myself. I kept receipts and recorded purchases using pen and paper before transferring the data to the spreadsheet daily or weekly. With months of spending data accumulated, I was able to identify where the hole in the bucket was. It was tons of small purchases, mostly made with debit cards or cash.

Often, small purchases were easy to overlook. But by tracking every expense down to the penny, I gained insight into our spending habits and realized that we needed to make changes in order to have money left at the end of each month—or even to simply pay our bills.

Categorizing expenses also helped me analyze our spending. Grouping expenses into different categories allowed me to not only track our spending but also see where our money was going. Some personal finance websites and credit cards even have automatic categorization features that can help identify spending themes. For example, I discovered that impulse buys at Target or recurring subscriptions like Spotify or streaming services were taking a toll on our finances.

Small purchases

In today's society, it's effortless to make numerous small purchases without even realizing it. We spend money in small amounts all the time, everywhere we go. Whether it's on coffee, snacks, sodas, fast food, or our children's needs, the list seems endless. However, our constant cash spending was causing a significant problem. By the end of each month, we had no money left.

This was surprising to both Tonya and me because we considered ourselves to be frugal. Whenever we made a purchase over $100, we would always stop and think carefully about it. Could we find it more cheaply elsewhere? Was it a good deal? Did we really need it? If I wanted to buy something that was more than $100, I would run it by Tonya first—unless I didn't want her to know about it. In those cases, I would try to act clueless and hope she wouldn't notice (which hardly ever worked).

Spending $100 or more was something we were cautious about. But when it came to purchases under $20, we didn't give them much thought at all. It was these smaller purchases that were like tiny holes in our checking account bucket.

Cash was my preferred method of mindless spending, but with modern technology, there are many other ways to deplete your accounts without even realizing it. Debit cards, credit cards, mobile payment options like Apple Pay, PayPal, and services such as Venmo, CashApp, and AfterPay have made it incredibly easy to spend but challenging to keep track of our expenses.

It turns out there's something called the "perception of cost," where small purchases are perceived as less significant financial commitments compared to large purchases. When spending small amounts, individuals often think, "It's just a little money," which can lead to a more relaxed attitude toward spending. This perception reduces the psychological barrier associated with spending money, making it easier to justify multiple small transactions. (25)

Plus, stores know we are susceptible to these small purchases, which often occur in environments designed to encourage impulse buying-such as checkout lines or discount stores. The convenience and accessibility of these items make it easy to add them to our cart without much thought, whereas larger purchases typically require more deliberation and planning.

Our brains actively work against us, rewarding our purchases with a release of dopamine. This chemical reaction is linked to feelings of pleasure and reward. Making multiple small purchases can intensify this sensation, creating a series of "mini rewards" that encourage the behavior. On the other hand, larger purchases may not elicit the same immediate gratification, causing hesitation or guilt about spending a significant amount all at once. (26)

More common than you think

One common issue I encounter when meeting with new clients is their misunderstanding of how money is spent. Many people think in terms of $100 increments instead of smaller, $20 ones. When discussing their larger problem of not having enough money at the end of each month, we often discover that these seemingly insignificant purchases add up over time. Some clients may initially resist or deny this as their true problem. In those cases, I use a tool to bring this issue to light.

I ask the couple to participate in an experiment: keeping a journal of their expenses for one week. They can use either a physical journal or their phone's notes app. Each time they make a purchase, they have to record the item and price. It may seem like a simple task, but surprisingly, most people don't complete the full week. The longest recorded time was three days. However, even after just a few days, the problem becomes glaringly obvious and can no longer be ignored. This is essential in finding a solution—recognizing the issue before trying to address it.

Once we understand what purchase we are making, it's important to ask ourselves the next question: Why? Why are we making these purchases? What do they mean to us, and what do we hope to gain from them?

For some, the answer may be simple and practical. They need a new car because their old one broke down, or they need a new computer because their old one is too slow. But for others, the answer may be more complex and emotional. Perhaps they want to impress their peers with their expensive clothes and gadgets, or they want to feel a sense of status and success by owning certain items. Or maybe they simply enjoy the rush of buying something new and shiny, even if they don't necessarily need it.

But often, the reasons behind our purchases are not so clear. They may be rooted in deep-seated insecurities, childhood experiences, or societal pressures. And sometimes, we may not even realize why we feel compelled to buy certain things.

It's important to stop and ask ourselves "Why?" before making any purchase, to truly understand our motivations and make sure they align with our values and goals. Otherwise, we may find ourselves chasing after empty fulfillment and constantly seeking external validation through material possessions.

CHAPTER 8

WHY WE BUY WHAT WE BUY

W e allocate a significant portion of our income toward necessary expenses such as housing and bills. However, beyond that, most of our spending is based on our personal choices, which reflect our values, habits, and emotional state. This is why the game of "justifying purchases" often leads to arguments. When we ask someone to justify their spending, we are essentially asking them to defend their core values. Sometimes, our spending can also serve as a way to deal with our fears or emotions. It's natural for us to become defensive when asked to explain and justify our choices. To overcome this reaction, it's important to recognize and understand our own emotional responses and where they stem from.

Are we overreacting because of an unrecognized fear that's driving our spending behavior? Is our partner trying to protect themselves and our family from a deep-seated fear of which they might be unaware? Is the husband assuming the relationship will be fine in the long run and neglecting the family's emotional needs? Is the wife focused on developing familial relationships without considering the financial and practical implications of those choices?

Those assumptions are an oversimplification, but they offer a starting point. They reflect different values and priorities that can clash when we talk about money matters. So much of the conflict and pain couples experience come from each person's internal fears and their attempts to avoid those fears as much as possible.

Luckily, it doesn't have to be all bad. These conversations can be a wonderful opportunity to deepen your connection with your partner. When we understand our partner's deep fears, we can do a better job of showing compassion and empathy. We can work through those fears together as partners in love rather than enemies in conflict. We can harmonize our values and priorities and, in the end, build a closer and more loving relationship.

Spending reflects our values

Ivan's story—spending reflecting his values

Ivan's spending habits were as predictable as the sunrise. Every morning, he would stop by the local café and order a small black coffee and a croissant, savoring the flaky layers and rich aroma. He would then make his way to the library, where he spent hours lost in the pages of classic literature, always returning the borrowed books on time to avoid late fees.

His simple and frugal lifestyle was a stark contrast to the lavish and ostentatious displays of wealth that surrounded him. Yet Ivan never faltered in his convictions, always choosing to spend his money on experiences rather than possessions. To him, books were the greatest luxury, transporting him to distant lands and introducing him to new perspectives. And his daily ritual at the café was a reminder to savor life's simple pleasures.

As he walked through the bustling streets, Ivan felt content with his choices, knowing that his spending habits were a reflection of his true values. He may not have had a large bank account, but he had a wealth of meaningful experiences that money could never buy.

Let's get one thing clear—spending money isn't inherently bad! Money is a tool we use to build the life we want to live, and we are all not like Ivan.

Anne's story—spending not reflecting her values

A perfect example of the murky gray area can be seen through my client, Anne. Initially, she expressed that her top priority was spending quality time with her family. However, when she came in one day and declared it was time for a change, she revealed how quickly priorities can shift in life.

As the sun set over the cityscape, Anne sat at her kitchen table sorting through her credit card statements with a sense of unease. The numbers and figures were all familiar, yet they seemed to mock her, exposing a truth she was not yet ready to face. Despite priding herself on being financially responsible and budget-conscious, the statements painted a different picture. They showed a pattern of spending that did not align with her professed values.

Although Anne wanted to believe that she valued family time above all else, her credit card statements told a different story. They revealed numerous purchases for expensive dinners out with friends, extravagant trips to far-off destinations, and indulgent spa treatments. It was evident that her true priorities did not match what she claimed to hold dear.

As she continued to examine the statements, a wave of regret washed over her. She realized that her spending habits not only reflected her values but also reflected her character. And she was not pleased with what she saw.

Feeling shame and disappointment, Anne acknowledged that it was time for a change. She would have to reassess her priorities and make conscious decisions about her spending in order to truly align her actions with her values. It was an intimidating task, but one that she knew was necessary for personal growth and development. As she closed the statements and put them away, she felt determined and hopeful for a better, more authentic future ahead.

Ben's story—buying experiences

There are different ways in which people spend money to feel good about themselves and their lives, depending on their values, preferences, and goals. Once way is to focus on experiences versus things.

The sun was setting over the horizon, casting a golden glow over the bustling city streets. Among the hustle and bustle, one man stood out with his serene demeanor and quiet grace. His name was Ben, and he lived his life by a simple motto: to buy experiences, not things.

As he walked down the street, he couldn't help but notice the endless rows of stores and shops, each one filled with material objects promising happiness and fulfillment. But Ben knew better. He had learned through personal experience that the key to true happiness lies not in possessions but in experiences.

So, instead of entering the stores and indulging in the temptation of material goods, Ben continued on his way to the airport. He had booked a last-minute flight to a country he had always dreamed of visiting, and he couldn't wait to immerse himself in the culture and learn about the people and their way of life.

As he boarded the plane, he couldn't help but feel a sense of excitement and anticipation. He knew this trip would bring him more happiness and fulfillment than any material thing ever could. And he was right. Over the next few weeks, Ben traveled through the country, learning new skills, tasting new foods, and making lasting memories. And with each passing day, he felt more connected to himself and the world around him.

As he boarded his flight back home, he couldn't help but smile at the thought that he had once again proven the research right— experiences truly do bring more happiness than material things. And for Ben, that was all he needed to live a truly fulfilling life.

Isla's story—spending on others

Donating to charity, buying gifts, or treating a friend to a coffee can boost your mood. Sharing your resources with others can increase your self-esteem and foster a sense of meaning and purpose.

Spending on others was second nature to Isla, a kindhearted woman with a generous spirit and a love for helping those in need. She found joy in donating to charities, buying gifts for loved ones, and treating friends to coffee or a meal.

On this particular day, as she walked through the bustling city streets, she couldn't ignore the urge to brighten someone's day. As Isla spotted a homeless man shivering on the sidewalk, her heart went out to him. She remembered how good it felt to receive a warm meal or a kind gesture when she was struggling, and she knew she could make a difference in this man's life.

Without hesitation, Isla walked over to the man and handed him a bag filled with sandwiches, a thermos of hot soup, and a few dollars. The man's eyes widened in surprise, and then softened with gratitude as he thanked her. Isla smiled and wished him well before continuing on her way.

As she walked on, Isla felt a sense of fulfillment and purpose wash over her. She knew that her small act of kindness had made a big impact on the man's day, and that thought brought her immense joy. And she couldn't help but think that if everyone shared their resources and showed compassion toward others, the world would be a much brighter place.

Expressing your self-identity

This includes buying clothes or accessories and participating in hobbies that reflect your personality, values, and interests. These pursuits help you feel authentic and self-confident.

It was a crisp spring morning when Emma first discovered her love for thrifting. The kind of morning where the sunlight filters through the trees, casting dappled shadows on the sidewalk. She was wandering aimlessly through the bustling streets, her mind a jumble of worries and insecurities. As she passed by a small, unassuming shop, a yellow sundress in the window caught her eye. It was the kind of dress that seemed to whisper her name, beckoning her inside.

The bell above the door tinkled as Emma entered, the musty scent of old clothes washing over her. The shelves were lined with a hodgepodge of items— vintage teapots, records, crochet doilies, and racks upon racks of clothes. She made her way to the dress, running her fingers over the soft fabric, feeling a sense of familiarity and comfort wash over her.

The shop owner, a kind-faced woman with gray hair and warm eyes, appeared at Emma's side. "That dress is from the 1960s," she said, a smile tugging at the corners of her mouth. "It's one of my favorites."

Emma couldn't resist trying it on, and as she stood in front of the mirror, admiring the way the fabric hugged her curves and the sunshine yellow brought out the freckles on her cheeks, something inside her shifted. For the first time in a long while, she felt like herself. Not the person she was supposed to be, or the person others wanted her to be, but the person she truly was—carefree, whimsical, and unapologetically her.

From that moment on, she was hooked. Emma combed through the racks, finding treasures and pieces of her identity hidden among the forgotten and discarded. There was something magical about the process—finding an item that spoke to her, giving it new life, and wearing it proudly as an expression of her true self.

Kate's story—spending money to increase free time

This means hiring a house cleaner, ordering takeout, or taking public transportation. This can reduce stress and free up your time for more enjoyable or meaningful activities.

Kate found herself breathing a little more easily this week. She had taken the advice of her therapist and started spending money to increase her free time. It was a foreign concept to her, having grown up in a frugal household where every penny was carefully accounted for and often stretched to its limit. But, as she had begun to realize, time was far more precious than money.

After a long day at work, Kate didn't want to come home and spend hours cleaning her small apartment or waste more time on a long commute just to save a few dollars. Instead, she hired a house cleaner to come once a week, freeing up her evenings for more relaxing and enjoyable activities. She also started ordering takeout instead of spending hours cooking elaborate meals and took public transportation instead of driving herself to work every day.

The result was a newfound sense of calm and balance in her life. Kate had more time to pursue her passions and hobbies, and more energy to invest in meaningful relationships. The extra money she spent on these conveniences was well worth the mental and emotional freedom she gained.

As she settled into bed each night, Kate couldn't help but feel grateful for the simple yet profound shift in her mindset. She no longer saw money as the be-all and end-all, but rather as a tool to enhance her life in ways that truly mattered. And for that, she was willing to spend a little extra.

Eliza—buying now, consuming later

This includes booking a vacation in advance, saving up for a big purchase, or buying a subscription service. This can create anticipation, excitement, and gratitude for future experiences or goods, which can be a powerful force—one that propels us forward with a sense of purpose and hope. With this kind of anticipation, we know that the reward will be worth the wait.

This is exactly what Eliza was doing as she sat at her desk, scrolling through travel websites and dreaming of her upcoming trip to Europe. She had been planning this trip for months, meticulously researching the best places to visit and budgeting every dollar she could spare. And now, with only a few weeks left until her departure, the excitement was building within her, like a fire waiting to be ignited.

As she clicked through photos of Parisian cafes and Italian cobblestone streets, she couldn't help but feel grateful for the opportunity to experience these things. She had worked hard for this trip, sacrificing her usual luxuries and setting aside every extra penny she could find. And now, the reward was almost within reach.

But it wasn't just the trip itself that excited Eliza. It was the knowledge that she had planned and saved for it, the sense of accomplishment that came with being able to afford something she truly desired. It was a reminder of her own resilience and determination, traits that she often doubted she possessed.

As she continued to research and plan, the anticipation grew stronger, fueling her excitement and gratitude for what was to come. And in that moment, she couldn't help but feel grateful for the concept of buying now and consuming later, for the lessons it had taught her and the experiences it allowed her to have.

How you spend

How you spend your money is up to you. It helps to be mindful of how your spending choices affect the happiness and well-being of you and your partner. As the saying goes, money can't buy happiness, but it can buy things that make you happy—if you spend it wisely.

Spending habits can reflect our values, but they also can reflect our fears or insecurities. It's a cruel twist of fate that our attempts to ease our own fears by spending money can unintentionally frighten our partners and cause their fear levels to rise. Let's look at some common ways both men and women spend money to alleviate internal fears.

How men use money to alleviate fears

Men and their money: a topic often fraught with tension and unspoken expectations. As with any generalization, there are bound to be exceptions, but societal and cultural norms have a way of influencing men's spending habits and financial decisions, particularly within a marriage.

Take, for example, the common expectation that a man should be the breadwinner in a relationship. This belief, rooted in traditional gender roles, can put pressure on men to earn more and therefore spend more, often leading to financial strain and stress within a marriage. On the other hand, some men may feel ashamed or emasculated if they're not the primary earner, causing them to overcompensate and spend more frivolously in an attempt to prove their worth. (27)

Additionally, societal expectations of masculinity can influence how men choose to spend their money. The need to appear strong, successful, and impressive can lead men to splurge on luxury items or experiences, even if they can't afford them. This can further exacerbate financial issues within a marriage, as one partner may be spending beyond their means in order to maintain a certain image. (27)

Of course, it should be noted that these patterns may not apply to every individual. Each person's relationship with money is unique, and societal expectations should not dictate how we choose to spend and save. However, being aware of these influences can serve as a starting point for open and honest discussions about financial matters within a marriage. (27)

Men often harbor fears and anxieties about their ability to provide for their families, which stems from societal pressures. As a result, they may spend money in ways that seem perplexing to their wives. Insecurities about success or self-doubt may drive some men to use spending as a means of boosting their social status.

For instance, purchasing expensive items could be an attempt to prove their worth and gain respect from others, especially their peers. A simple hobby like golf could turn into a costly affair as they strive to have the best equipment, clothes, and memberships in order to impress others. Even something as basic as a car purchase can be driven by the need to show off their success rather than practicality. Ultimately, men's desire to appear successful is rooted in deep-seated emotions.

Actions rather than words

Society expects men to be stoic, unemotional creatures, so they often turn to actions rather than words to express their innermost feelings. This is especially true when it comes to money, a tangible and quantifiable form of emotion that can be easily exchanged. For some, making grand gestures with their wealth is a way to demonstrate love or affection, while for others, it may be a means to assert dominance or control.

In this patriarchal society, where men are taught to bury their emotions and instead focus on material success, money becomes a substitute for emotional expression. It's a tool that can be used to convey love, anger, pride, or any other sentiment that may be difficult to articulate. But this behavior isn't limited to gendered expectations; it's also a reflection of broader cultural and psychological patterns. In a world where material possessions are often equated with happiness and success, it's no wonder that men use money as a proxy for emotional expression.

Through this lens, we can understand the actions of a man who showers his lover with expensive gifts as a way to compensate for his inability to say "I love you." Or the businessman who lavishly spends on his family to make up for his absence due to work obligations. Even those who use money as a means of control may be doing so because they lack the emotional intelligence to communicate their feelings in a healthy way.

It's a complicated dance, this interplay between money and emotions, but it's a dance that has become deeply ingrained in our societal norms and individual tendencies. And so we see men using money as a tool to express themselves, whether consciously or subconsciously, in a world that often requires them to suppress their emotions. (28)

Expressing love through saving

Men may use money to enhance their self-esteem by saving and investing a lot, or by splurging on their family and satisfying their desires. Think back to Simon and Michelle—Simon spent his money on housing and financial security, expressing his love and care through investment in a financially secure future. Saving for the future is great, but not if it's rooted in insecurity and comes at the expense of your relationship.

Coping with insecurities: financial success as self-worth

Money can be tied to self-esteem and identity for men. Being able to spend money or provide financially can alleviate insecurities about self-worth and competence, especially in the context of relationships. (29)

Jason sat at his desk, surrounded by stacks of paperwork and a computer screen filled with numbers and charts. He had spent the majority of his life pursuing financial success, equating it to his self-worth and identity as a man. Growing up in a family where money was scarce and his parents constantly struggled to make ends meet, Jason knew from an early age that he never wanted to experience that kind of insecurity. He saw how money could have alleviated stress and provided a sense of security and stability in his parents' relationship.

As he grew older and began working in the corporate world, Jason quickly climbed the ladder, working long hours and sacrificing personal relationships in pursuit of financial success. It became his way of proving his worth and competence to himself and those around him. He felt a rush of pride and accomplishment every time he received a promotion or a raise, and his self-esteem skyrocketed with each new financial milestone.

But despite his achievements and impressive bank account, Jason still carried insecurities about his self-worth. And so, he continued to chase after more money, believing that it would somehow fill the void and prove his worth once and for all. He couldn't bear the thought of losing his job or experiencing any kind of financial setback, as it would shatter his carefully constructed identity.

As he sat at his desk, surrounded by the trappings of his success, Jason couldn't help but wonder if it was all worth it. Was this really who he was, defined by his bank account and career achievements? Or was there more to life than just financial success? He couldn't shake off the gnawing feeling that perhaps he had been chasing after the wrong things all along.

Our fears and insecurities can be triggered not only by our own spending, but also by how our family chooses to spend money

Shopping with my daughter

When my daughter reached her senior year of high school, she developed a love for thrift stores. She and her friends would scour consignment shops for vintage or used clothes (which I referred to as hand-me-downs) and proudly show them off at school. I couldn't quite grasp the appeal, and chalked it up to being too old to understand. I grew up shopping at secondhand stores, but not by choice. The rich kids shopped at the mall, while my family put new school clothes on layaway and waited until the last minute to make the final purchase.

As a parent in my 50s, I couldn't quite understand the appeal of this trend, and it brought up bad memories. However, one day my daughter convinced me to go to a thrift store with her. The store was huge, clean, and crowded with people hunting for deals.

My daughter's excitement over thrift shopping only grew with each visit. She would eagerly snatch items from the racks and drop them into her cart with abandon, barely taking a second glance at the price or brand name.

Despite the incredibly low prices (think $3 for a shirt or $7 for a jacket), I couldn't shake off the stress and anxiety that consumed me. It was unsettling to find myself, someone who had always strived to provide for their family, reduced to buying secondhand clothes at a thrift store, just like when I was growing up.

As I stood there feeling like a fish out of water in the sea of bargain hunters, I couldn't help but marvel at the range of emotions a thrift store could evoke in me. Here I was, navigating through aisles of pre-loved treasures like a lost dog in a maze of discounted dreams. As my daughter eagerly picked out items to purchase, I couldn't help but feel like a failure—though I kept that to myself.

What I really wanted to do was shout to everyone: "Hey, we're not poor, we can buy new clothes no problem, this is just my daughter's hobby!" I'm sure that would have gone over well. Perhaps I could have formed a support group for bewildered parents dragged into thrift shopping by their fashion-savvy offspring.

In the end, as I sat in the car waiting for my daughter's fashion conquests to be tallied up at the checkout counter, I couldn't help but chuckle at the absurdity of it all. Who knew that a trip to the thrift store could be such an emotional roller-coaster ride? And hey, at least now I knew where to go if I ever needed a vintage Hawaiian shirt!

How women use money to alleviate fears

Just as with men, not all women share the same spending habits or emotions. Again, these are patterns I've observed in my own life and with my clients; every person and every relationship is different!

Some women may use money to achieve **independence and security**. They may have worked hard to earn money and pursue their dreams and may not want to depend on anyone else for their financial well-being. They may use money to protect themselves from uncertainty, risk, or hardship. This relates to the **gender wage gap** of income, wealth, and opportunities that women still face in many areas of life, as well as the relative recency of women's financial independence. According to the U.S. Bureau of Labor Statistics, women's earnings were 83.6 percent of men's in 2023. (30) In addition, according to the *Industrial Psychiatry Journal*, financial security is a significant factor in **emotional well-being**. Economic independence can provide women with the confidence and stability needed to feel secure in their personal and professional lives. (31)

Teresa's Story

Teresa is a client of mine who had worked tirelessly to achieve her dream of financial independence. She had watched her mother struggle for years, including being divorced three times and becoming trapped in a cycle of dependency on men. Teresa had told me that, long ago, she had decided she would never end up like her mother, relying on a man to provide for her.

So, she worked multiple jobs, saved every penny she could, and sacrificed any luxuries for the sake of her independence. It wasn't easy, but it was worth it to Teresa. She refused to let herself be tied down by societal expectations or the constraints of traditional gender roles.

At our first meeting, she expressed her desire to meet with an advisor and create a plan for making her hard-earned savings grow and ensure she had enough saved for retirement. She told me that when she sat at her desk in her house, the one she had finally made her own, a wave of pride and fulfillment washed over her. Despite her mother's constant doubts and criticisms, Teresa had achieved exactly what she'd set out to do. She was in control of her own life, with her own aspirations and ambitions, and she had accomplished them all independently. Her mother's voice lingered in her mind, but Teresa knew she had proved her wrong.

I'm sure she couldn't help but feel grateful for the journey she'd taken. It had been tough, but it had also shaped her into the fierce and independent woman she was today.

Some women may use money to **express values, identity, or creativity**. They may have a strong sense of what's important to them and how they want to live their lives, and may use money to support those causes and interests. They also may use money to express their personal style, spending it on things that reflect who they are and what they enjoy. This relates to the **gender socialization** process by which women learn the behaviors, roles, and norms that society expects based on their gender. This process begins at a very early age and continues throughout life, influencing how women perceive themselves and interact with the world—where women are taught to be expressive, empathetic, and cooperative. (32)

Some women may use money to **fulfill this role**. They may feel obligated to maintain a certain beauty standard for themselves, including clothing purchases, personal care appointments, or other similar services, and/or maintain a high standard of household management. This includes styling a safe, comfortable home for themselves and their family, both in day-to-day life and when hosting important events. This relates to the **gender roles** men and women play, in which women are expected to be more submissive, nurturing, and supportive. (32)

Mom guilt

One of my clients, a young mother of three, opened up to me about her struggles with "mom guilt." She shared how she constantly felt torn between investing in her own health and well-being and spending that money on her children's needs. She felt like she was being selfish if she chose to take care of herself, even though she knew that doing so would ultimately benefit her family.

It's a common theme among mothers— this self-sacrifice and putting their children's needs above their own. But what many fail to realize is that taking care of oneself is not a selfish act. It can actually lead to a more emotionally satisfied and present mother, which in turn benefits the entire family.

As I listened to my client speak, I couldn't help but wonder why it was so ingrained in our society for mothers to put themselves last. Why is it seen as a badge of honor to sacrifice their own needs for the sake of their children? Shouldn't it be encouraged for mothers to invest in their own well-being, both for their own sake and for the sake of their families? These were questions I couldn't answer, but they lingered in my mind as I continued to listen to my client's struggles with "mom guilt." And I couldn't help but admire the strength and selflessness of mothers, even as I hoped for a society that would support and encourage them to prioritize their own well-being.

Retail therapy

One difference between how women and men spend money is in retail therapy. Retail therapy, also known as shopping therapy, is the practice of shopping with the purpose of improving one's emotional state or mood. This behavior often occurs during times of stress, sadness, or anxiety when individuals find solace in purchasing items—referred to as "comfort buys."

Retail therapy can be described as using shopping as a means to reduce stress, feel better, boost mood, or satisfy compulsive urges. Although retail therapy is not a substitute for actual therapy, it can offer a temporary boost in mood as long as it's done in moderation.

Shopping has become an integral part of modern life, whether you enjoy spending hours browsing in stores or prefer the convenience of online shopping. Many people have experienced the uplifting feeling that comes from making a purchase while feeling down or stressed. The act of shopping can induce positive emotions because it provides a sense of control that counters feelings of powerlessness, sadness, stress, or anxiety. According to WebMD (33), making decisions about purchasing items can help individuals feel empowered and in control of their choices, which may offset any negative feelings they are experiencing. Whether they decide to make a purchase or not, the act of choosing allows for a sense of agency and empowerment in the midst of overwhelming emotions

Things to keep in mind

There's no shame in using retail therapy to cope with stress or sadness from time to time. But if you know you tend to go shopping when you've had a rough day, keeping the following tips in mind can help you continue to see benefits from retail therapy—*without* harm.

Stick to your budget

Most people would consider overspending and debt the primary negative consequences of retail therapy. To avoid this hazard, budget for your spending. Set aside some money to use for retail therapy each month, then keep to that limit.

If you want to shop when you've already reached your spending limit, create a plan to save up for something you want. Saving for a desired item can feel rewarding, too, and so can using restraint when you're tempted to shop.

The bottom line

Itching to treat yourself? In most cases, there's no need to deny yourself. Retail therapy really *can* help you feel better, as long as you don't overspend. But remember, retail therapy isn't actually therapy.

If you're experiencing mental health symptoms or you're struggling with a serious problem, talking to a therapist can have more benefits than pulling out your wallet.

Shopping versus buying

One female client of mine told me: "Men go 'buying,' women go 'shopping.' There's a big difference." I finally understood this when I took a trip to Florida with Tonya to see some of our friends. When we arrived at our rented vacation house and settled in, all the husbands wanted to go see all the sights, a.k.a. watch the game at one of the beach bars. The wives wanted to go shopping.

In the saga of husbands' vs. wives' vacation dynamics, it seemed like the battle of "buying" vs. "shopping" took on a life of its own! While the guys were busy contemplating the intricacies of beach bar menus and debating which game to watch, the women embarked on their epic shopping quest. It was like a tale as old as time—the husbands seeking out cold drinks and sports highlights, while the wives roamed the stores in search of treasures and bonding moments.

As the women proudly displayed their purchases, maybe they were secretly showcasing their triumphant victory in the eternal game of "Who Can Have More Fun?" Surely, the guys must have felt a twinge of jealousy as they gazed upon those bags filled with potential friendship points. Who knew that a simple shopping excursion could hold such power, turning mundane transactions into priceless relationship investments!

So, next time you find yourself torn between joining the guys at a bar or accompanying the ladies on a shopping spree, remember there's more to retail therapy than meets the eye. It's not just about bags and shoes; it's about building connections, sharing laughs, and maybe snagging a killer deal or two. And who knows, you might just end up with a newfound appreciation for thrift shopping—courtesy of my daughter's wise ways!

Partnership

After understanding the reasons and motives behind our purchases, it should be clear that we all have unique needs and desires when it comes to spending money. As a man, I would often seek items that conveyed a sense of success and competence as a way to prove my worth in the world. My wife, on the other hand, would use shopping as a form of therapy, self-expression, or creativity—a way to temporarily escape from the pressures of daily life and indulge in things that made her feel good.

But then it became time for us to put our differences aside and work together as a team. We needed to manage our finances and create a united plan for our future, one that would benefit both of us and our family.

We should have felt a sense of relief and peace. Finally, we were on the same page, working toward a common goal. We should have felt a newfound sense of trust and camaraderie with each other, knowing that we were in this together, no matter what.

CHAPTER 9

MANAGING MONEY

We resist being fully one in our marriage, and it shows in our finances

Let's start by discussing how you and your partner manage your finances on a day-to-day basis. Do you have a joint bank account, or do you keep separate bank accounts and have a specific arrangement for paying bills, like one person taking care of the mortgage while the other handles utility expenses? Or perhaps you have a different system in place, where one person covers certain expenses while the other takes care of others?

Meet Martin and Amelia

Money was always a touchy subject for them, filled with past resentments and unresolved issues that only added more strain to their already fragile relationship. They had learned to avoid talking about it altogether, choosing instead to maintain separate bank accounts and divide up expenses. Amelia was responsible for the mortgage, while Martin covered utilities and groceries. Any additional costs were split evenly between them. This approach seemed to work at first glance, but deep down, they both held onto feelings of resentment and suspicion toward each other's spending habits. Martin couldn't help but question why Amelia always seemed to have the latest gadgets and designer clothes, while Amelia didn't understand why Martin refused to treat himself to a nicer car or a vacation.

These unspoken judgments and accusations weighed heavily on their relationship, but neither of them wanted to address them. So, they continued with their established roles, avoiding any discussions about their finances as much as possible. It was a delicate balance that could easily be disrupted, but for the sake of maintaining peace and harmony, they chose to stick with it.

Unity

In my role as an advisor, I can observe how people handle their finances, and it reveals a lot about their hearts. It shows me what truly drives them—what they're thinking and feeling deep down. The way a couple manages their money speaks volumes about the state of their relationship. Keeping separate accounts may seem like a practical decision, but it can also indicate a lack of true unity between partners. We all have some level of selfishness within us, and if we let it grow unchecked, it will manifest in our financial decisions.

Therefore, in marriage, we must confront these issues head on and be vulnerable with our spouse. Trust and communication are key components in achieving true oneness. It may feel risky to expose ourselves completely to another person, but the rewards are worth it. Purposefully changing our approach to money and focusing on what truly matters can bring about positive changes in our heart and our relationship. It's natural to want independence and separate accounts, but true happiness in marriage comes from being one in all aspects of life. This can be challenging, as we are imperfect beings, but by trying to protect ourselves we may actually be driving a wedge between ourselves and our partner.

There are various ways to manage finances and accounts within a marriage, but ultimately, it's important to consider the intentions behind each person's actions. Unity and oneness should always be the ultimate goal. There are many obstacles that can hinder unity, such as not wanting someone else to tell us what to do or feeling like the other person is wrong. Some individuals struggle with trust or value their independence above all else. These reasons may lead to them keeping separate finances or avoiding financial dependence on a spouse.

Unity requires a shift in mindset: "I am still an individual, but I am now part of something bigger." We must acknowledge the natural inclination to resist merging with another person and actively work against it. This involves prioritizing what truly matters and consistently acting in accordance with that. We must also have faith in our spouse's genuine intentions toward us and actively seek out evidence of their love and support.

For a marriage to thrive, we must push back against these impulses that pull us away from unity, and strive toward becoming one with our partner. It takes effort and compromise, but the reward of a strong and united partnership is well worth it.

Checking account with a twist

When working with clients, I always stress the importance of a couple having a shared vision for their finances and unity within their spending habits. However, I also understand the need for some personal independence in day-to-day purchases. Don't get me wrong—there should be a common goal for retirement, funding education for children, setting monthly budgets, and staying debt-free. But it's also important to have freedom in making personal purchases without consulting your partner every time. For example, if my wife wants to spend money on her nails or clothing, we don't need a financial meeting. Similarly, if I want to buy clothes or sporting goods, I can make that decision without setting up a Zoom call. Of course, there should still be boundaries and budget restrictions around how much we can spend. But what really makes this work well is setting aside a specific amount each month for our personal spending needs.

Creating your financial infrastructure

In order to successfully manage and track your finances, it's important to set up a solid financial infrastructure. This involves establishing a primary checking account where all of your paychecks will be deposited, along with two additional "slush" accounts.

The first step is to open your primary checking account. This account will serve as the hub for all of your financial activity. It's where your paychecks will be deposited and where you'll pay your bills from. Make sure to choose an account with no fees that offers perks like online bill pay, mobile banking, and ATM access.

Next, you'll want to set up two additional "slush" accounts—one for you and one for your partner. These accounts can be used for any personal expenses throughout the month, such as dining out or buying clothes. As stated earlier, the idea behind these accounts is that each partner has some money designated specifically for their personal spending needs without having to consult the other person every time they want to make a purchase.

It's important to determine how much money should go into these slush accounts each month. This will depend on your individual budget and spending habits, but it's important to have a clear understanding of how much you can spend without jeopardizing your overall financial goals.

Now that you have your financial infrastructure set up, it's crucial to keep track of your spending and stay within budget. Consider using budgeting apps or spreadsheets to help monitor your expenses and stay on track.

Another helpful tip is to schedule regular check-ins with each other about finances. Set aside some time once a month (or more frequently if needed) to review your budget, discuss any upcoming expenses, and make adjustments if necessary. For example, if your main account will be short of funds one month, then your slush accounts will be smaller or nonexistent for that month.

As Tonya and I have become experts in our use of the slush account system over the years, we've mastered the art of budgeting and saving. One strategy I like to employ is setting aside an entire month's worth of "slush" funds so I can make a bigger purchase the following month. It also gives me some satisfaction to show off my "large" purchase to Tonya, who always marvels at how I managed to do it. On one occasion, I found myself short on funds for a desired purchase, but instead of having to wait until the next month as planned, Tonya generously offered to dip into her own slush fund to help me out. She's the greatest.

By creating this financial infrastructure, you can ensure that you're both on the same page when it comes to managing your money while also allowing for personal independence in spending choices. This sets a strong foundation for achieving shared financial goals and maintaining a healthy financial relationship.

How to save money, when there's no money left?

The weight of money is a burden that many choose to ignore, until the moment it becomes too great to bear. For most, it is the daily, seemingly insignificant purchases that add up and drain the bank account, rather than one large expense. A morning coffee, a lunch out with coworkers, a quick trip to the convenience store for a snack—all these small transactions add up quickly, but they seem so insignificant in the moment.

It's easy to get caught in this cycle, to let our money slip away in drips and drops without even realizing the toll it is taking. We continue to make these small purchases, barely giving them a second thought, until suddenly we're faced with the fact that we're not saving any money and are forced to confront the reality of our spending habits.

It's as if our bank accounts are leaking water, but we're so used to the constant dripping that we hardly even notice. However, when we're faced with a large hole, we finally have to acknowledge the problem and take action.

We must learn to be mindful of our spending, to plug the leaks before they become too great. It's not an easy task, but it is a necessary one if we want to have control over our financial stability.

With the ease of making small purchases, it's important to find ways to stop, and to instead start saving money for our future or creating an emergency fund. One method is to use brute force: create a budget, track expenses, set specific savings goals, and hold yourself accountable. I've personally attempted this approach in the past, with limited success. I've also tried to guide others in their efforts, but have seen only moderate progress. A lot of success or failure depends on the motivation of the individual.

Creating a budget and tracking expenses is a common approach to saving money and cutting back on unnecessary spending. It involves listing all sources of income and all expenses, and then finding ways to reduce or eliminate certain expenses in order to save more money. However, this method often fails because it relies on willpower and discipline alone. It can be difficult to stick to a strict budget, especially when faced with temptations or unexpected expenses.

Another approach is to focus on the bigger picture and set specific savings goals. This can help shift our mindset from immediate gratification to long-term financial security. For example, saving for a dream vacation or a down payment on a house can motivate us to cut back on daily indulgences.

But setting goals alone is not enough. We also need to have a realistic plan in place for achieving those goals. This may involve creating multiple streams of income or finding ways to save money through discounts, coupons, or negotiating with service providers.

One effective strategy that combines both these approaches is the envelope system. This involves dividing cash into different envelopes labeled with specific categories, such as groceries, dining out, entertainment, etc. Once an envelope is empty, there can be no more spending in that category until the next month.

This method forces us to be mindful of our spending and can make it easier to stick to our budget and savings goals. It also allows for some flexibility, as we can choose how much money goes into each envelope each month based on our priorities.

Our mindset working against us

When examining the issue through the lens of money psychology, we can see that there are numerous obstacles standing in our way. Our emotions, including fear, pride, and overconfidence, can greatly impede our ability to effectively handle and save money. These feelings may cause us to put off important financial tasks or develop unhealthy spending and investing habits: (34)

- **Impulse control and emotional spending**: The inability to resist immediate gratification and emotional spending can result in unsustainable financial habits. This often involves spending money to cope with emotions rather than necessity. (35)

- **Mindset and beliefs**: Personal beliefs about money, often shaped by our upbringing and cultural influences, can impact our financial behaviors. For instance, a scarcity mindset may lead to excessive frugality, while an abundance mindset might encourage risk-taking. (36)

- **Cognitive biases**: Cognitive biases, such as loss aversion and mental shortcuts, can affect our financial decision-making. These biases may lead us to avoid beneficial financial opportunities or make irrational spending choices. (34)

A better way

There is a method—a financial philosophy, if you will—that tackles both our psychological blocks and our difficulty in keeping track of every expense and aligning it with a monthly budget while still being able to save money. This process is known as Pay Yourself First.

It's a simple concept, really, but one that's straightforward and works very well. The idea is to set aside a certain amount of your income for savings before you even pay your bills or indulge in any discretionary spending. By making yourself a priority and treating savings as a necessary expense, you ensure that you always have money stashed away for the future.

For some, this may seem counterintuitive or even impossible. But the truth is, when we prioritize savings, we are forced to live within our means and be more conscious of our spending habits. We become less likely to overspend on frivolous things and more likely to stick to our budget. And as we watch our savings grow, we feel a sense of accomplishment and security, knowing that we have a safety net for the unexpected.

Making a habit of paying yourself first can lead to financial stability. It's an age-old philosophy that still holds true today, and one that we should all strive to integrate into our lives. A budget is like a car—it can take you to a stronger financial future, but it needs fuel to run. That fuel is Pay Yourself First. It's the key to successfully budgeting, saving, and achieving financial success. From my experience working with hundreds of families, I've seen firsthand how Pay Yourself First has greatly benefited many of them in their financial journeys.

The magic

Before entering the financial services industry, my idea of achieving financial success was based on selecting a winning investment, saving more than spending, or simply getting lucky. Little did I know how complex the world of finance truly was. If someone had told me that the key to prosperity was as simple as "paying yourself first," I would have dismissed it or even argued against it. How could such a basic concept be more effective than investing early in companies like Microsoft or Amazon?

But the magic behind Pay Yourself First is that it tackles three core money behaviors: uncontrollable spending, the inability to save, and emotional decision-making when it comes to money. By addressing these obstacles, you gain a significant advantage in working towards financial freedom. The beauty of this system is that it doesn't rely on willpower. It works with your human nature instead of against it.

Pay Yourself First means prioritizing protecting your future self above all else. This mindset removes the notion that savings are leftover money and instead makes it a top priority. Then, by separating your funds into different categories based on your values and goals, you remove your emotions from every decision. And best of all, this method naturally curbs impulsive spending without relying on willpower.

The first bill you pay

Do you remember the bill monster that constantly loomed in mine and Tonya's kitchen? The solution is not to try and remove it all at once, but to prioritize which bills to pay first. And surprisingly, the first bill you should focus on isn't one from an external source—it's for your own future: your protection and savings. After allocating funds toward your emergency and savings accounts (more on those later), whatever's left can be used to tackle your pile of bills and any other purchases. Then, once you've paid into these designated "buckets" and made progress on reducing your debt, the remaining money goes into your checking account to cover all other expenses until your next paycheck.

I can already anticipate your objections: "But you said we don't have enough money because our checking accounts are leaking! How will we manage after paying into these accounts?"

The answer is simple. You may not have enough cash for every small purchase, but the holes in your budget will start to close themselves as you prioritize saving and paying off debts and go into "lean mode."

Lean mode

We all have the ability to get "lean" or not spend money for a few days—typically at the end of the month, when all our money is gone. We can "stretch" a small amount of money to make it last a little longer than we might typically be comfortable with. We can't do this all month long, but we can for a short amount of time. It's like sprinting versus a marathon—you can push a little harder the last 50 yards.

By paying yourself first, you'll know when you need to be more frugal with your money. You'll know how much money you have left with a quick glance at your account balance. You'll know the important bills—your savings—are already accounted for. If your balance is low and you still have a few days until your next check, you'll naturally switch to "lean mode." You'll stop grabbing coffees and eating out. You'll make a weird batch of chili with whatever vegetables are left in the fridge. Lean mode isn't forever—it's just until you get paid again. Lean mode requires that you only spend the money you actually have! It doesn't work if you're spending carelessly with credit cards—which isn't spending, it's borrowing.

With Pay Yourself First, you don't have to rely on a budget that never worked. You don't have to mentally calculate how much money you've spent on Starbucks this month while you're standing at the door to the coffee shop. You don't need to look at an app, or track your purchases as you make them. You just need a quick glance at your account balance every now and then.

Early in our marriage, saving at the end of the month never worked for Tonya and me because we always spent more than we planned to. We had no reason to go into lean mode, because the money was still there in our account balance. So, it was easy to save nothing and spend everything. If I saw there was money in the account near the end of the month, I would find something to spend it on—and if I saw we were running short, we would go into lean mode.

Pay Yourself First works because you save first, then adjust your spending accordingly.

Unexpected expenses

Things happen. That's life. Sometimes a car breaks down, or the water heater needs replacing, or your kid chucks a baseball through the neighbor's window. Pay Yourself First doesn't require life to be perfectly predictable all the time. This is why your first savings bucket should be your emergency fund. It will grow every month until you have between six and nine months of expenses, and you shouldn't feel guilty for dipping into it when you have real emergencies. But your emergency fund isn't a restaurant fund— not wanting to cook dinner at the end of the month is not an emergency. You know who you are.

Help—I'm broke!

Sometimes, your income is too low and your expenses are too high. What do you do if you "pay yourself first" and then don't have enough money to live your life?

Well, you were living this way before you started paying yourself first, and it wasn't working for you. Maybe you were digging yourself into a debt hole or living paycheck to paycheck with no savings at all. If you don't have enough money to support yourself after paying yourself first, that's a very important data point to have. Having that knowledge is the first step toward financial stability. You can't fix the problem if you're in denial about it!

First, you need to identify if the problem is short-term or long-term. If you just need to get through a few tight months, a side gig may be the way to get through. By "side gig," I mean a short-term way to make a little bit of extra money. For example:

- Sell things (like sports gear or home goods) that are collecting dust in your home on eBay or Facebook Marketplace.

- Drive for Uber, Lyft, or food delivery services like DoorDash or Instacart.

- Tutor online via Chegg, Wyzant, or TutorMe.

- Complete surveys or tasks online via Swagbucks, InboxDollars, or Amazon Mechanical Turk.

- ... or use your imagination to find a way to make a little money off your unique skills or hobbies.

If, every month, you still don't have enough money despite going into "lean mode" or looking at side hustles, you should focus on long-term solutions. Look at long-term lifestyle solutions that seriously cut your expenses, such as changing your transportation or housing, or focus on increasing your income and take steps to change your career—or do both. You could pursue additional job training, go back to school, or change careers entirely. None of these long-term solutions is easy, but the road to financial freedom is long, too. If Pay Yourself First informs you that your income is too low, and you're ready to fix that, you're already off the hamster wheel and heading in the right direction.

Pay-Yourself-First with a budget

Pay Yourself First is a useful tool for managing your finances and staying within your budget. However, it shouldn't be used as a replacement for a budget; rather, it should complement it. Creating a personal financial budget has many benefits that contribute to financial stability and reaching goals. A budget allows you to monitor your income and expenses, preventing overspending and promoting responsible financial habits. It also serves as a roadmap for pursing specific financial goals, such as saving for a vacation or paying off debt. Budgeting will help you establish an emergency fund, providing security during challenging times. It also helps you keep track of debts and prioritize repayments to effectively manage them.

By having a clear financial plan, you can reduce anxiety related to money management and improve your mental well-being. Evaluating your spending habits through budgeting can lead to more mindful spending, allowing for better allocation of resources toward essential needs and savings. Asset allocation does not ensure a profit or protection against loss.

Overall, maintaining a personal financial budget is crucial in taking control of your finances, and pursuing your goals, preparing for emergencies, managing debt, and reducing financial stress. Regularly reviewing and adjusting your budget is necessary for ongoing financial health and success.

Picture this

As the sun set behind the horizon, casting a warm golden glow over the rooftops of the city, Stella sat at her kitchen table with a stack of bills in front of her. She had always been careful with her money, making sure to budget and save for a rainy day. But in recent months, her expenses had started to outweigh her income and she knew it was time to take action.

Taking a deep breath, she began to create a personal financial budget. She listed all of her monthly expenses, from rent to groceries to utilities, and calculated how much she could realistically spend in each category. Then, she added up her total income and subtracted her expenses, leaving her with a small surplus that she could put toward savings.

As she looked at the numbers on the page, a sense of relief and control washed over her. She knew that by sticking to this budget, she could get her finances back on track and avoid falling deeper into debt. And as she folded the paper neatly and placed it in a binder, she couldn't help but feel a sense of pride for taking control of her own financial well-being.

Creating a personal budget may seem like a tedious task, but for Stella, it was a necessary step toward securing her future. And as she closed her eyes and drifted off to sleep that night, she knew she was one step closer to pursuing her goals and living a financially stable life.

How to create a budget that actually works

Creating a personal budget involves several key steps:

1. **Calculate your net income (how much comes into the checking account):** Determine your total take-home pay after taxes and deductions.

2. **Track your spending:** List all your monthly expenses, including fixed costs (rent, utilities) and variable expenses (groceries, entertainment).

3. **Set financial goals:** Establish short-term and long-term financial objectives, such as building an emergency fund or saving for retirement (more on this later)

4. **Categorize your expenses:** Divide your spending into essential (needs) and nonessential (wants) categories.

5. **Choose a budgeting method:** Consider using the 50/30/20 rule (50% needs, 30% wants, 20% savings) or another budgeting strategy that works for you.

6. **Record and analyze your spending:** Keep track of all expenses for at least a month to get an accurate picture of your spending habits.

7. **Adjust your spending:** Look for areas where you can cut back if necessary to align with your financial goals.

8. **Review and adjust regularly:** Revisit your budget monthly or quarterly to ensure it remains accurate and aligned with your goals.

9. **Use budgeting tools:** Consider using budgeting apps, spreadsheets, or other financial tools to help you track and manage your budget more effectively.

10. **Use percentages, not just dollar amounts:** Looking at your spending as a percentage of your income can provide better insights into your budget allocation

11. And of course, involve your partner, ensuring both of you are on board with the budget and spending limits.

Remember, a successful budget should be realistic and flexible. It may take some time to find the right balance, but consistently tracking your income and expenses will help you gain control over your finances and work toward your financial goals.

Next, let's take a look at where to put all that hard-earned money you're going to save. Because let's face it, you didn't work that extra shift and skip your daily latte just to let it sit in a checking account earning next to nothing in interest. You want that money to work for you, to grow and multiply.

CHAPTER 10

INTRODUCING THE BUCKETS

*"Money is like manure. You have to
spread it around or it smells."*

—*J. Paul Getty*

W e've made significant progress thus far. We've gained insight into our own and our partner's perspectives on money, making communication easier and more constructive. We've also come to the mutual understanding that having a shared checking account for bill payments is necessary, while setting aside some personal funds for individual expenses is beneficial. Additionally, we've recognized the importance of prioritizing saving with the Pay Yourself First method, which allows us to effectively manage our finances and stick to a budget. However, this approach should not be utilized as a substitute for having a budget; rather, it should complement it.

In this chapter, we'll explore what happens to our money after we get paid and the potential consequences of leaving it in our checking account.

Leaving money in our checking account may seem like a safe option, as it will be easily accessible for everyday spending. However, there are risks associated with this approach. If left unchecked, the balance may dwindle without us realizing it. This can lead to overspending and difficulty keeping track of our expenses.

Another issue with keeping all our money in a checking account is the lack of growth potential. Checking accounts typically offer very low interest rates, or none at all, meaning that our money is not working for us and may even lose value due to inflation. Moreover, having a large sum of money in a single account may make us vulnerable to fraud and theft. Hackers and scammers often target checking accounts as they are connected to debit cards and can provide immediate access to cash.

To avoid these potential issues, it's important to have a plan for what happens to our money after we get paid. This plan should include strategies for saving, and investing our money in order to pursue our financial goals. By implementing these strategies, we can make sure that our hard-earned money is working for us rather than sitting stagnant in a checking account.

Buckets

Instead of thinking about my checking account, emergency fund, short-term savings, and retirement accounts separately, I like to imagine them as different financial buckets. This makes it easier for me to visualize and manage my finances.

I suggest setting up five separate accounts, but the final number is ultimately up to you. Each bucket will represent a different area of saving, and the buckets should not be combined or used interchangeably. Just as you would create a separate account for a vacation fund at your bank, these buckets should have their own designated purpose and be kept separate from your checking account.

Automation is crucial for the success of this plan. As I mentioned earlier, it's not wise to rely on your self-control when it comes to limiting small purchases throughout the month. Similarly, you can't rely on yourself to remember to transfer money from your checking account to designated savings or spending categories; it's unlikely that you'll remember or prioritize this task. The key is automating the process so it happens automatically as soon as you receive your paycheck.

Here is a list of the buckets:

- Checking account
- Spouse slush accounts
- Emergency fund
- Short-term savings account
- Retirement account

With each paycheck, a portion of your earnings should be allocated to each designated fund.

In order to effectively manage your financial buckets, it's important to have a clear understanding of how much money is going into each one. This requires creating a budget and allocating a certain percentage or dollar amount to each bucket with every paycheck.

- **Checking account:** This is where the majority of your paycheck should go. It covers your daily expenses such as rent/mortgage, bills, groceries, transportation, etc. Ideally, you want to keep just enough in this account to cover these expenses for the month.

- **Spouse slush accounts:** If you are married or have a partner, it's important to each have a separate account for any personal expenses or discretionary spending. This can help avoid disagreements over money and ensure that both partners have equal access to funds for personal spending.

- **Emergency fund:** This bucket should contain at least three to six months worth of expenses in case of unexpected events such as a job loss, a medical emergency, or major home repairs. It's important to prioritize building up this fund before focusing on other savings goals.

- **Short-term savings account:** This bucket should be used for short-term goals such as saving for a down payment on a house, buying a car, or taking a vacation. The amount allocated to this fund will depend on your specific goals and the timeline for achieving them.

- **Retirement account:** Finally, it's important to allocate some portion of your paycheck toward retirement savings in order to secure your financial future. The exact amount will vary depending on your age and retirement goals, but it's recommended to aim to save at least 10–15% of your income in this bucket.

By automating these allocations with every paycheck, you can ensure that each bucket is consistently being funded without having to rely on self-control or remembering to transfer money manually.

While it may appear overwhelming to create and manage multiple accounts, once the initial setup is done, the process will practically run itself with minimal tweaks over time. This approach also enables you to monitor your progress toward each objective and make necessary changes as needed.

In a previous chapter, we covered the checking account and spouse slush accounts. Now, let's focus on the other three buckets: emergency fund, short-term savings, and retirement bucket.

Emergency fund

An emergency fund is a savings account specifically set aside for unexpected financial emergencies or expenses. Here's why you need one:

- **Build a financial safety net:** An emergency fund acts as a buffer against unforeseen circumstances, providing you with financial security and peace of mind.

- **Avoid debt:** Having an emergency fund helps you avoid relying on high-interest credit cards or loans when unexpected expenses arise, preventing you from falling into debt.

- **Cover unexpected costs:** This fund can be used for surprise expenses like medical bills, car repairs, home appliance replacements, or sudden job loss.

- **Maintain financial stability:** An emergency fund helps you maintain your financial stability during challenging times, reducing stress and preventing long-term financial setbacks.

- **Quick access to funds:** Emergency funds are typically kept in easily accessible accounts that allow you to withdraw money quickly when needed—like a savings account at the same bank you have your checking account.

- **Protect your long-term savings:** By having a dedicated emergency fund, you avoid tapping into your retirement savings or other long-term investments for short-term emergencies.

Experts generally recommend saving three to six months worth of living expenses in your emergency fund. However, even starting with a smaller amount, like $500, can provide a helpful financial cushion. The Certified Financial Planner (CFP) Board emphasizes that you shouldn't feel intimidated by the target amount. Instead, they recommend looking at your budget and deciding how much you can realistically allocate to emergency savings each month. (37)

Short-term savings bucket

This is my favorite bucket, and often the most overlooked! Most people recognize the importance of saving for emergencies, and some people recognize the importance of saving for retirement, but most people forget to save up for something delightful. Make sure you save for something that'll make your heart speed up a little! Your money should work for you and bring you joy.

I encourage my clients to have some fun with this one and choose a bucket-worthy quest!

- **The exotic family vacation bucket:** Imagine whisking your kin off to a land where kangaroos serve tea and palm trees hum lullabies. A place so far-flung that even your GPS gets lost. Yes, my friends, this is where you save for that family vacation to a locale so extraordinary, your neighbors will raise their eyebrows and say, "They went WHERE?!"

- **The new home or new car bucket:** Ah, the sweet smell of fresh paint in a brand-new abode! Or the thrill of gripping a shiny steering wheel, knowing you've upgraded from the "Rusty Relic" to the "Zoom-Zoom Deluxe." It's leveling up in the game of life, my friends.

- **The mystery bucket:** This one's for the rebels, the dreamers, the ones who secretly want to build an outdoor entertainment area or create a new art studio in their house. Whatever floats your boat— or bucket—go for it!

The short-term savings bucket does not need to be something as dramatic as a vacation or a new car. It can also be used for more immediate, fun goals, such as:

- A new set of family bikes for exploring local trails with the whole family

- Matching team jerseys with your family to represent your team in style

- LASIK eye surgery to enjoy the beach without constantly cleaning your glasses

- National parks annual pass for amazing weekend trips at a low cost

- Couple's massage session... because you deserve it for all your hard work setting up your finances!

This savings journey will likely require a timeframe of a year or more. Investing the money may be an attractive option, but the challenge is the unpredictability of the market over such a relatively short period. The thought of saving diligently each month for a specific goal only to watch your account lose value simultaneously can be disheartening. This naturally leads to the inclination to opt for "safe" options like savings accounts or money market accounts.

Retirement Buckets

According to the CFP Board, the general recommendation for retirement savings is to aim to save 15% of your gross income. Specifically:

- This 15% includes any employer match on retirement contributions, if available.

- For young savers, the CFP Board suggests considering funding a Roth IRA after capturing any available employer match on a 401(k). Once the contribution limit on the IRA is reached, they recommend returning to the 401(k) to maximize contributions there.

- This 15% savings goal is considered a priority after establishing a starter emergency fund and paying off high-interest "toxic" debt.

- The CFP Board emphasizes that this retirement savings should be prioritized even before fully building out an emergency fund or paying off lower-interest debts.

It's important to note that this 15% guideline is a general recommendation. Individual circumstances may require you to adjust this percentage up or down based on factors such as age, current savings, and retirement goals. The CFP Board encourages working with a financial professional to determine the most appropriate savings rate for your specific situation. (38)

Other buckets: College

Aside from the buckets mentioned above, it may also be worth considering setting up an education savings bucket if you have kids or are thinking about furthering your own education in the future.

Many families have the major financial goal of saving for future college costs and other educational expenses. Luckily, there are several tax-advantaged savings programs that can help with this, such as 529 plans, Coverdell education savings accounts, and custodial accounts. According to the CFP Board, it's essential to start saving for a child's college education as early as possible. They emphasize that there is no such thing as starting too early. (39)

Although saving for college may potentially impact eligibility for financial aid, the CFP Board believes it is still worth doing. They encourage parents to assess their budget and determine a realistic monthly amount they can allocate toward college savings. Working with a CFP® professional can also be beneficial in understanding and maximizing different education savings options, according to the CFP Board. (40)

The CFP Board stresses the importance of creating a person-alized savings plan based on your individual circumstances and goals. Seeking guidance from a financial professional can help you determine the most appropriate savings strategy for your unique situation. (39, 40)

Building a financial plan

While the bucket system is helpful in managing finances, my intention in writing about it was to assist couples in building strong communication skills around money matters. The end goal is for them to work together with a financial advisor and create a personalized financial plan tailored to their individual needs.

There are several important reasons to build a financial plan:

- **Maximize potential for meeting life goals:** The CFP Board defines financial planning as a process that "helps maximize a Client's potential for meeting life goals through Financial Advice." (42) A financial plan is designed to help you achieve what you want in life, not just your financial goals.

- **Integration of personal and financial circumstances:** Financial planning integrates "relevant elements of the Client's personal and financial circumstances." (41) This holistic approach considers how different aspects of your life and finances interact and affect each other.

- **Address multiple financial aspects:** A comprehensive financial plan can help you manage various financial elements, including "assets and liabilities, cash flow, identify and manage risks, identify and manage the financial effect of health considerations, provide for educational needs, achieve financial security, preserve or increase wealth, identify tax considerations, prepare for retirement, pursue philanthropic interests, and address estate and legacy matters." (41)

- **Increased confidence and security:** According to a survey by the CFP Board, 96% of financial advisors agree that clients become more confident and secure about their financial futures when they have a cash flow management plan in place. (42)

- **Long-term perspective:** Financial planning encourages a long-term view of finances, which can help reduce short-term anxieties about money. (42)

- **Improved decision-making:** A clear financial plan provides a framework for making informed financial decisions, reducing uncertainty and associated stress. (42)

- **Adaptability to changing circumstances:** The CFP Board emphasizes that financial planning is an ongoing process, and allows for adjustments as your life and financial situations change. (41)

- By building a financial plan, you're taking a proactive approach to managing your finances, which can lead to greater financial stability, increased confidence, and the ability to achieve your life goals.

Certified Financial Planner (CFP®)

I believe in transparency, so I suggest that you seek out and collaborate with a Certified Financial Planner (CFP®). Just to be clear, I want to disclose that I am also a CFP®, but there are many others who hold this certification. You can easily find one through the CFP Board website, and I highly recommend working with one for your financial planning needs.

Benefits of working with a CFP®:

- **Comprehensive financial planning:** CFP® professionals take a holistic approach to financial planning, assessing clients' entire financial situation and developing personalized strategies for areas like retirement planning, investment management, tax optimization, and estate planning. (43)

- **Higher client satisfaction:** Clients working with CFP® professionals report 87% satisfaction, compared to 72% satisfaction for clients of non-certified financial advisors. (44)

- **Fiduciary duty:** CFP® professionals are committed to acting as fiduciaries, meaning they are ethically bound to act in their clients' best interests. (44)

- **Expertise and experience:** CFP® professionals undergo rigorous education, training, and examination to earn their certification, ensuring they have comprehensive knowledge in various aspects of financial planning. (43)

- **Ongoing support and guidance:** CFP® professionals provide regular check-ins on progress toward financial goals and help clients make smarter financial decisions. (45)

- **Customized financial planning:** CFP® professionals develop tailored financial plans that consider clients' unique goals, risk tolerance, and financial circumstances. (43)

- **Improved financial management:** CFP® professionals can provide guidance on budgeting, cash flow management, debt management, and tax minimization. (43)

- **Long-term perspective:** CFP® professionals help clients develop and maintain a long-term view of their finances, which can reduce short-term anxieties about money. (46)

- **Ethical standards:** CFP® professionals adhere to a strict code of ethics and professional conduct set by the CFP Board. (43)

Overall, working with a CFP® professional can provide clients with comprehensive personalized financial guidance that goes beyond just investment advice, helping them achieve greater financial security and confidence in their financial future.

Ok, now that you've suffered through my commercial, let's look at the problem of debt.

CHAPTER 11

DEBT—THE GOOD, BAD, AND UGLY

The very word "debt" evokes uneasiness in most people. It holds a great deal of influence over our lives, but it doesn't have to be a negative force. In fact, with proper management, we can use debt to our advantage.

But what exactly is debt? How do we end up in debt and, more importantly, how can we break free from its grasp? And once we are liberated from its clutches, how do we ensure that we stay out of debt for good?

This chapter will delve into the intricacies of debt—its origins, and the steps we can take to regain control of our financial life. Drawing on personal experiences, expert insights, and extensive research, I will provide a comprehensive guide on understanding and overcoming debt.

Understanding debt is a complex challenge. It would be easy to say that all debt is bad, but then none of us would own homes! Debt cannot be classified as simply "good" or "bad." Rather, it's a tool with both benefits and drawbacks depending on how we use it.

Effectively managing debt is like walking a narrow path up a mountain. If we veer too far to one side and believe that all debt is terrible and must be eliminated, we may miss out on opportunities to grow our wealth. On the other hand, if we lean too heavily toward believing that all debt is good and should be leveraged to increase wealth, we risk falling deep into a debt hole. As with most things in life, the key lies somewhere in between. That's how we reach the top of the mountain. Our goal is to understand when, where, and how to use debt as a tool and do our best to minimize its negative effects.

Almost everyone will encounter debt at some point in their lives. It often starts accumulating during college with credit card debt, and then grows with car loans, student loans, mortgages, and medical bills. I've seen clients struggle with debt well into retirement. To build a solid financial future, we must closely examine our debts and assess how they are impacting our lives.

So, let's embark on this journey together, and by the end, hopefully we will have a deeper understanding of debt and the tools to break free from it. Even if you're not currently dealing with debt and credit issues, there is valuable information in this chapter that can help you effectively manage your finances, increase your income, and use your money toward more fulfilling activities. This includes:

- Differentiating between "good debt" and "bad debt" and why taking out loans for things like mortgages, student loans, or business ventures can actually benefit us in certain situations
- Student loans, credit cards, mortgages, and other types of debt
- How to pay off debt and stay out of debt

Once you have a better understanding of debt, you can confidently assess your own financial situation and come up with a plan or reach out to a financial advisor for assistance. This chapter will guide you in creating a personalized path toward financial security. You will learn how to manage different types of debt, whether that involves cutting back on expenses or finding additional sources of income through side jobs. By effectively managing your debts, you can achieve financial freedom and work toward your goals, such as having a financial cushion, owning a home, or saving for retirement.

Facing our debts head-on can alleviate the stress of managing our finances. It allows us to pay off monthly bills without worry and build up savings for any unexpected circumstances. With a clear understanding of debt, we gain financial confidence, which helps us overcome challenges and create a comfortable nest egg.

Let's start with how loans work

A loan requires a legal agreement between two parties, typically involving paperwork and signatures. It commonly involves a bank or another entity lending money to an individual. The process often includes stacks of documents on a desk, filled with numbers and complex terminology. These contracts may be signed confidently and boldly, or with hesitation and uncertainty.

At its core, a loan is simply borrowed money that must be repaid in the future with additional interest (extra money). While most loans come with more conditions and features, they essentially involve a promise to return something valuable. There are always two sides to a loan: the lender and the borrower. The lender provides something, usually money, to the borrower, while the borrower agrees to repay what was borrowed plus an added bonus (whether it be extra funds, livestock, or days of labor) for the lender's benefit.

Being **"in debt"** means owing money to someone else. It can come in different forms, such as loans, credit card balances, mortgages, and other types of financial responsibilities. Often, debt comes with interest, which is the fee for borrowing money from a lender. While debt itself is not necessarily negative, it can become burdensome when it becomes too much to handle.

You are not alone

The numbers on the screen seemed to blur together, a never-ending string of digits representing the mountains of debt held by American consumers. The figures seemed to grow by the second, a disheartening reminder of the financial burden carried by so many. Based on the latest data Americans have significant amount of debt across various categories:

- **Total household debt:** Americans have a record total household debt of $17.80 trillion as of Q2 2024. (47) This represents an increase of $109 billion from the previous quarter.

- **Credit card debt:** Credit card debt reached an all-time high of $1.142 trillion in Q2 2024. (48) The average credit card debt per American is $6,501 as of Q3 2023. (48) Credit card debt saw the largest increase of any debt category, growing by 16.6% between Q3 2022 and Q3 2023. This was partly due to more people carrying balances month to month and increased retail spending. (48)

- **Mortgage debt:** Mortgage debt accounts for the largest portion of household debt at $12.519 trillion. (48)

- **Other types of debt:**
  - ○ Auto loan debt: $1.626 trillion (48)
  - ○ Student loan debt: Not specified in the given data, but it's a significant component
  - ○ Other consumer debt (including retail cards and other loans): $2.129 trillion (48)
- **Average household debt:** The average American household debt in 2023 was $104,215. (48)
- **State variations:** Credit card debt varies significantly by state. **Alaska** has the highest average credit card debt at $7,863, while **Kansas** has the lowest at $5,227 (49)

This data shows that Americans are carrying substantial debt across multiple categories, with credit card debt and mortgages being particularly significant components of overall household debt.

History of debt

In the time before money was created, people would barter to fulfill their needs. Each trade was a simple exchange, with no debts or credits involved. However, the introduction of currency (long before it actually existed) changed everything. The concepts of debt and credit were born over 5,000 years ago and ever since have played a dominant role in how people manage their finances.

The concept of money existed even before coins and paper currency were introduced. As far back as 9000 B.C.E., sheep and cows were used as forms of payment by different societies around the world. Some even used cowrie shells, beads, or feathers. But this "money" wasn't used for shopping; instead, it was used to settle disputes and arrange marriages.

As civilizations developed, merchants emerged as a new class of people. People began buying and selling goods and services, with most transactions related to agriculture. Soon, the concept of credit and debt came into existence as customers started purchasing on credit and paying later.

The first evidence of debt appeared in 3500 B.C.E. in Mesopotamia, where merchants would record debts on clay tablets that were confirmed by borrowers' personal seals. These debts were often used as a form of currency for trade purposes. In 1754 B.C.E., the Code of Hammurabi was established, which laid out regulations regarding credit and debt. Written contracts with witnesses became necessary for loans, and interest rates were capped (for example, grain interest could not exceed 33%). Borrowers were also required to provide collateral such as land, houses, livestock, or family members (yes—family members) to assure lenders that they would repay their debts. If borrowers were unable to pay their debts, such as a farmer whose crops were destroyed by a natural disaster, they often fled their homes. This became so common that kings started offering amnesty to debtors, returning their property if they couldn't pay. (50)

Credit card growth and kudzu

Consumer debt has grown exponentially, resembling the pesky weed kudzu, which just won't stop spreading. In previous times, people would take out loans to buy homes and purchase goods from local merchants on credit, but this was never seen as a major issue. However, with the introduction of the first universal credit card (Diners Club) in 1950, consumer debt took on a new form.

Initially, credit cards were considered charge cards, meaning the full balance had to be paid off immediately. But in 1958, Bank of America changed the game by launching the first revolving credit card (BankAmericard) in California. Within a decade, this card went nationwide, and consumers across the country began accumulating credit card debt.

Types of debt

Debt comes in various forms, but they can be categorized into two main types. One is **secured loans**, which involve borrowing against goods like a home or jewelry. This means that if the borrower fails to pay back the loan, the lender has a way of getting their money back. The other type is **revolving or unsecured loans**, which refers to whether the loan amount remains constant or can change, allowing for more borrowing on the same loan. These factors play a role in determining the interest rate of the loan.

- **Secured debt:**
    - Backed by collateral (e.g., a house or car)
    - Examples: mortgages, auto loans, secured credit cards
    - Generally has lower interest rates due to the reduced risk for lenders
- **Unsecured debt:**
    - Not backed by collateral
    - Based on the creditworthiness of the borrower
    - Examples: credit cards, personal loans, student loans, medical bills
    - Usually has higher interest rates than secured debt

- **Revolving debt:**
  - Provides a line of credit that can be repeatedly borrowed from and repaid
  - Examples: credit cards, home equity lines of credit (HELOCs)
  - Allows for flexible borrowing and repayment
- **Installment debt**:
  - Loans repaid in fixed installments over a set period
  - Examples: mortgages, auto loans, personal loans, student loans
  - Often has fixed interest rates and predictable monthly payments
- **Mortgage debt:**
  - Used to purchase real estate
  - Typically long-term loans (15–30 years)
  - Can be fixed-rate or adjustable-rate
- **Credit card debt:**
  - Revolving, unsecured debt
  - Often has high interest rates
  - Requires minimum monthly payments
- **Student loan debt:**
  - Used to finance education
  - Can be federal or private loans
  - Often has special repayment options

- **Auto loan debt:**
  - Used to purchase vehicles
  - Typically secured by the vehicle itself
- **Personal loan debt:**
  - Can be secured or unsecured
  - Used for various purposes (e.g., debt consolidation, home improvements)
- **Medical debt:**
  a. Resulting from healthcare expenses
  b. Often unsecured, and may have flexible repayment options

Understanding these different types of debt can help us make informed decisions about borrowing and manage our finances more effectively.

Secured versus unsecured

When something is secured, it is protected from harm or danger. In the case of a loan, securing it means that the lender is not at risk of losing their money. This is why they are willing to lend it to you: their fear of loss has diminished. Even if you have a good track record of repaying loans and your word is trustworthy, this does not guarantee that a loan will be secured. Things like unexpected medical emergencies, job loss, or even impulsive decisions could result in an inability to repay the loan. If there is nothing tangible for the lender to take as collateral, they stand to lose the money they lend you.

In its basic form, collateral refers to something that exists alongside something else. In the world of finance, collateral is property that is promised to the lender or given to them as a guarantee for the loan. This property does not have to be directly related to the loan, although it often is. For instance, when taking out a car loan, the lender will often place a lien on the vehicle. This property serves as security for the lender's money and will be returned once the loan is repaid in full.

Pawnshops are a perfect example of this concept. You bring in a valuable item, like a diamond pinky ring your uncle Pawley gave you, and the broker loans you $250. When you pay back the loan (plus interest, of course), you get your ring back. However, if you fail to repay the loan, the broker keeps your ring. Essentially, you no longer own the ring, but you also don't owe any money. The transaction is finished, except for having to explain to your uncle why you no longer possess the ring.

For those who have taken out loans, it is essential to prioritize paying off secured debts when faced with financial constraints. While these payments may consume a larger portion of your budget, they are crucial to avoid losing important assets such as your home or vehicle, which will be taken by the lender if payments are not made consistently.

Some creative uses of collateral

Several amusing and unusual items have been used as collateral for loans, showcasing the creativity and sometimes absurdity of borrowers:

- **Soccer stars:** A Spanish bank used two players from Real Madrid, Cristiano Ronaldo and Ricardo Izecson dos Santos Leite, as collateral for a loan that totaled over $111 million. If the loan was not repaid, the players' contracts would have been transferred to the Central Bank of Europe. (51)

- **Cheese:** In Italy, some lenders accept wheels of artisan Parmesan cheese as collateral for business loans. This quirky practice highlights the value placed on high-quality cheese in certain markets. (51)

- **Designer handbags**: Upscale pawnbrokers have begun accepting designer handbags, sunglasses, and other luxury items as collateral for short-term loans, reflecting the growing trend of valuing fashion items. (51)

Unsecured debt

Unsecured debt doesn't come with the security of collateral. Here, the lender is banking on your ability and willingness to make all of the scheduled payments. Examples of unsecured debt include:

- Student loans
- Credit card debt
- Personal loans
- Medical bills

Approval process: Lenders typically rely more heavily on the borrower's creditworthiness, credit score, and promise to repay when approving unsecured loans.

Interest rates: Unsecured debts often have higher interest rates than secured debts due to the increased risk for lenders

Consequences of default: If a borrower defaults on unsecured debt, the lender cannot immediately seize any property. However, they may take other actions like reporting to credit bureaus, sending the debt to collections, or filing a lawsuit

In terms of debt classification, **payday loans** are considered unsecured loans. However, this may not be entirely accurate. Although borrowers do not pledge any physical assets, such as a car or a house, to the lender, they are required to provide direct access to their paychecks when they are received through methods like post-dated checks or Automated Clearing House (ACH) withdrawals.

While unsecured debt doesn't put specific assets at risk, failing to repay can still have serious consequences, including damage to your credit score and potential legal action by the lender.

Revolving loans versus nonrevolving loans

Revolving and nonrevolving are terms that describe the way money is borrowed. Revolving credit appears as a never-ending cycle, with money being borrowed and repaid repeatedly. Nonrevolving credit, on the other hand, consists of one lump sum borrowed and paid back in fixed installments.

Revolving Loans

Revolving loans, like credit cards and HELOCs, have a flexible balance that changes based on your financial activity. You can borrow up to a certain amount at any given time, and your monthly payments will vary depending on how much you've borrowed. This type of debt is called "revolving" because you can borrow the same money multiple times. As you pay off your debt, your available credit increases, but as you borrow more, it decreases. Although there is a maximum credit limit, you can still borrow more than that over time. Revolving debt can be secured, such as a HELOC tied to your house, or unsecured, like credit card debt.

Here are the key points about revolving debt:

- It has a preset credit limit that you can borrow against repeatedly.

- As you repay the borrowed amount, your available credit is replenished.

- You're only required to make minimum monthly payments, though you can pay more.

- Interest is charged on any unpaid balance carried over to the next billing cycle.

- Common examples include:

  1. Credit cards

  2. Personal lines of credit

  3. HELOCs

- It's different from installment loans (like mortgages or car loans), which have fixed repayment terms.

- Revolving accounts typically have variable interest rates.

- Your credit utilization ratio on revolving accounts can significantly impact your credit score.

- Revolving debt offers flexibility in borrowing and repayment, but it can lead to ongoing debt if not managed carefully.

- It's considered an open-ended credit account, as there's no set date by which the entire balance must be repaid.

The key characteristic of revolving debt is the ability to repeatedly borrow, repay, and borrow again—as long as you stay within your credit limit and make at least the minimum required payments. (52)

Nonrevolving loans

Nonrevolving loans involve borrowing a specific amount of money at once and paying it back according to a predetermined schedule. These loans are structured and predictable, with set payment amounts and designated payoff dates. If more funds are needed, the borrower must go through the loan process again.

Examples of nonrevolving debt include car loans and mortgages. Typically, the outstanding balance of a nonrevolving loan decreases over time, except in cases of negative amortization, when unpaid interest is added to the total amount owed. Nonrevolving debt can be secured or unsecured depending on the circumstances. (53)

Predatory lending

Unscrupulous lenders prey on vulnerable or uninformed borrowers. They may present themselves as helpful, but their main objective is to make the most possible profit by loaning large amounts of money at exorbitant interest rates. They have little concern for whether the borrower can actually manage the debt based on their current financial state. In fact, they often target individuals who are struggling financially. As a result, these borrowers become trapped in a harmful cycle of debt and suffer from severely damaged credit. Many even lose their homes. (54)

Despite appearing to be illegal, predatory lending is not always punishable. While the federal government provides some protection, only 25 states have specific laws against it. (55) Many lenders exploit loopholes in the system, while others outright break the law. It's crucial to safeguard yourself and your finances by recognizing warning signs and refusing loans from predatory lenders, even if you're in dire need of money. Borrowing from these lenders will only worsen your situation.

Signs of predatory lending

Signs of predatory lending include a range of deceptive and unfair practices aimed at benefiting the lender at the borrower's expense. Here are some common warning signs:

- **Too good to be true offers**: If a loan offer seems too good to be true, it probably is. Predatory lenders may promise unrealistically low interest rates or guaranteed approval without considering your credit history.

- **Lack of transparency on costs**: Predatory lenders often fail to disclose the full costs of a loan, including the annual percentage rate (APR) and hidden fees. A reputable lender will provide clear information about all costs associated with the loan.

- **High interest rates and fees:** Excessive interest rates, especially those in the triple digits, and high fees are common indicators of predatory lending. These can trap borrowers in a cycle of debt.

- **Pressure tactics:** Predatory lenders may use aggressive sales tactics, such as rushing you to sign documents without giving you time to review them thoroughly.

- **Short repayment terms:** Loans with very short repayment terms can be difficult to pay off and may lead to additional fees if the borrower needs to extend the loan.

- **No credit check required:** Offering loans without assessing the borrower's ability to repay, such as skipping a credit check, is a red flag. This often leads to higher interest rates and fees.

- **Negative amortization and balloon payments:** Some predatory loans may include terms like negative amortization, where the loan balance increases over time, or balloon payments, which require a large sum at the end of the loan term.

- **Encouragement to borrow more than needed:** Suggesting that borrowers take out more credit than they need or can afford is another sign of predatory lending.

These practices can severely impact borrowers, leading to financial distress and difficulty in repaying the loan. It's crucial to be vigilant and thoroughly review all loan terms and conditions before committing to any financial agreement. (56)

How to protect yourself

To protect yourself from aggressive sales tactics by lenders, consider the following strategies:

- **Take your time:** Don't let lenders rush you into making a decision. If you feel pressured, take the loan documents home and review them thoroughly before deciding.

- **Understand the terms:** Ensure you fully understand all loan terms. If anything is unclear, ask for clarification. Avoid signing any documents if the terms are incomplete, confusing, or contradictory.

- **Shop around:** Compare offers from multiple lenders to find the best deal. This includes comparing interest rates, fees, and loan terms.

- **Learn to say no:** Be firm in declining offers that you're not comfortable with. Don't feel obligated to accept a loan just because a lender is persistent.

- **Beware of gifts:** If a lender offers you gifts or incentives to sign a loan, remember that you are under no obligation to accept the loan.

- **Keep your emotions in check:** Avoid making decisions based on emotions. Conduct thorough research and consider the long-term implications of the loan.

- **Consult experts:** Talk to a certified housing counselor or financial advisor for guidance. They can help you spot predatory lending practices and provide advice on the best loan options.

- **Check the lender's reputation:** Look up the lender in the Consumer Financial Protection Bureau's complaint database and on the Better Business Bureau website to see if there are any red flags.

By following these steps, you can better protect yourself from aggressive sales tactics and make more informed financial decisions. (57)

CHAPTER 12

NOT ALL DEBT IS BAD— HOW AND WHEN TO BORROW

W hen it comes to borrowing money, there are multiple options available. You may be seeking extra funds to consolidate debt, pay off medical bills, buy a home, buy a car, or take a vacation. The right choice for you will depend on your current financial situation. Ideally, the best time to borrow money is when you don't necessarily need it but choose to do so. This means that you are in a stable financial position with a strong credit score and a high net worth (particularly if you have valuable assets that can be quickly converted into cash).

In this scenario, lenders will compete to offer you loans at very low interest rates. With no immediate expenses to cover, you can use these loans as leverage to build your wealth more quickly by investing in productive assets with steady income potential or the opportunity for significant growth in value.

Borrowing versus debt

Debt can have a major impact on your financial situation, but the type of debt matters greatly. Good debt involves investing in assets or improving yourself, with the goal of increasing your net worth or your ability to grow it. On the other hand, bad debt lowers your net worth and puts your current and future financial stability at risk. This type of debt is often used for purchases that don't add value to your overall savings or income. Some forms of debt fall in between, such as car loans, and cannot be easily classified as good or bad.

Being aware of these distinctions can help you make smarter choices when borrowing money. However, don't be too hard on yourself if you take on some bad debt; it's nearly impossible to avoid it entirely. The important thing is to minimize it and pay it off quickly before it becomes overwhelming for your finances.

Good debt

Good debt can be compared to a well-designed blueprint, mapping out a path toward future wealth and success. It's viewed as a smart investment rather than a burden, with a specific purpose and end goal in mind. Good debt works in your favor, helping you achieve important milestones, increase your income, and improve your overall financial standing. This type of debt typically comes with lower interest rates and more favorable payment terms, which can positively impact your net worth.

However, taking on too much "good debt" can have negative consequences on your finances. It's crucial to avoid accumulating more debt than you can manage without straining your budget. This is especially important to consider for student loans, as many young individuals may enter into them without fully understanding the potential long-term effects on their finances.

Student loans

Taking out loans for your education is considered "good debt" because it's an investment in yourself and your future. However, the degree program you choose is vital in this discussion. If part of your education is funded through loans, it's crucial that the degree leads to a career with the potential to generate income. Otherwise, the debt can quickly become overwhelming.

The key factor in keeping student debt manageable is the amount you borrow. Instead of asking, **"How much can I get in student loans?"** the more important question is, **"How much can I realistically pay back?"** As a general guideline, it's best to borrow no more than what you expect to make as a starting salary after graduation. In fact, borrowing less is even better for keeping these loans affordable.

Here are some key guidelines for how much student loan debt you should take on:

- **Borrow only what you need:** Don't take out the maximum amount available just because you can. Only borrow what's necessary to cover your educational costs after exhausting other options like scholarships, grants, and savings.

- **Consider your future earning potential:** A general rule of thumb is to limit your total student loan debt to no more than your expected annual starting salary after graduation. Research typical salaries in your intended career field.

- **Calculate your future monthly payments:** Use a student loan calculator to estimate what your monthly payments will be after graduation based on different borrowing amounts. Make sure the payments will be manageable on your expected post-graduation budget.

- **Aim to keep federal loan borrowing within federal loan limits:** For dependent undergraduates, this means no more than $31,000 total in federal loans. For independent undergraduates, the limit is $57,500. (58)

- **Be cautious about private loans:** Federal loans offer more protections and flexible repayment options. Only consider private loans after maxing out federal options.

- **Consider the return on investment:** Evaluate if the degree you're pursuing and the school you're attending are worth the debt you'll be taking on. Will it lead to career opportunities that justify the cost?

- **Have a repayment plan:** Before borrowing, understand your repayment options and have a strategy for how you'll manage payments after graduation.

The key is to borrow conservatively and strategically. Take on only as much debt as necessary to achieve your educational goals while setting yourself up for financial success after graduation. Carefully evaluate the long-term implications of your borrowing decisions. (58, 59)

Attending college may require you to work a part-time job to minimize the amount of student loans you take out. This could potentially prolong your time in school, but this is a common measure taken by many students—including yours truly.

Home mortgage loans

Your mortgage will most likely be the biggest "good" debt you ever acquire. These loans are an efficient way to become a homeowner and to build equity in a property that will generally increase in value over time. However, as these loans can amount to hundreds of thousands of dollars, it's crucial to thoroughly comprehend the loan terms and interest rate and how they'll impact your financial situation in the present and future. It's important to consider your budget and avoid being lured into taking out a larger loan than you can comfortably afford.

Mortgage debt in the U.S., 2023

It's worth noting that mortgage debt has been steadily rising since 2013, with increases in home prices and interest rates accelerating growth, especially since the pandemic. (61) The total mortgage debt figure represents a record high for the United States (60):

- **Total mortgage debt:** As of Q2 2024, the total mortgage debt in the U.S. had reached $12.519 trillion. (60)

- **Average mortgage debt per borrower:** The average mortgage balance in America grew to $244,498 in 2023, an increase of $8,000 from 2022 (61)

Small business loans

Securing funding for a business can lead to a more stable financial future, where your success is dependent on your own hard work and determination. With determination and some luck, you can transform your business into a steady source of income for your family and a means of funding your retirement when the time comes. The key to maintaining this type of loan is beginning with a comprehensive business plan, regardless of whether you're just starting out or expanding. By knowing precisely how you'll utilize the funds to grow your company, your chances of achieving success increase exponentially.

Bad debt

Taking out a loan to cover nonessential expenses, or things you desire but don't necessarily need, falls under the category of bad debt. This also includes high-interest loans, even if they're used for necessary expenses, because they end up making everything two or three times pricier than if you'd paid for them upfront. This can create a dangerous cycle of relying on loans to cover your basic monthly needs, making it extremely difficult to break free from their grip.

As Jane sat at her kitchen table, staring at the pile of bills in front of her, she couldn't help but feel overwhelmed. She'd always known that she was living beyond her means, but in the moment, it all seemed so real and suffocating. The credit card statements, the loan repayments, the collection notices—they all felt like weights on her shoulders, dragging her down.

She had tried to convince herself that she needed these things, that they were necessary for her happiness and well-being, but in the end, they were just unnecessary extravagances. She couldn't believe how easily she'd fallen into the trap of relying on loans and credit to fund her lifestyle. And now, she was drowning in debt, struggling to keep up with the payments and the interest that seemed to grow bigger every day.

Sighing, Jane reached for her pen and started going through the bills one by one, calculating how much she owed and how much she needed to pay off each month to get out of this hole. As she did, she couldn't help but think about how different her life would be if she'd just lived within her means—if she'd been more responsible with her money.

But it was too late for regrets now. All she could do was buckle down and start paying off this bad debt, one payment at a time. It was going to be a long road, but Jane was determined to escape this vicious cycle and start living a more financially responsible life.

Credit card debt

It's important to understand that owning a credit card and having credit card debt are two different things. Credit card debt occurs when you have an outstanding balance that cannot be paid off in one lump sum.

Owning a credit card, a seemingly harmless piece of plastic that grants access to a world of endless spending possibilities, is a rite of passage for many young adults. It symbolizes independence, responsibility, and the promise of a brighter future. But little do they know that owning a credit card and having credit card debt are two vastly different things.

Credit card debt is a looming beast, a monster that threatens to consume its victims whole. It's the result of an outstanding balance that can't be paid off in one lump sum, and it's considered the most harmful type of debt for three main reasons.

Firstly, the high interest rates attached to credit card debt can quickly spiral out of control, making it almost impossible to catch up and pay it off. It's like trying to run up a steep hill with a boulder tied to your back. Every step forward is met with resistance, dragging you back down and further into debt.

Secondly, the payment schedules for credit card debt are carefully crafted to keep you trapped in a cycle of debt. Minimum payments are designed to barely cover the interest, without making a significant dent in the actual debt. This means that even if you're making payments, you're still accumulating more debt and staying in the same financial state.

Lastly, credit card debt is often used to purchase goods or services with diminishing value. It's easy to justify buying a fancy dinner or a new outfit with a credit card, but these items soon lose their appeal and leave you with only the debt to show for it.

Eliminating credit card debt is crucial for improving your current financial state, securing long-term finances, and increasing overall net worth. But it requires discipline, sacrifice, and a long-term plan. For many, it's a daunting task, but one that has to be tackled in order to achieve financial freedom

How credit cards work: the danger of plastic

For many individuals, credit cards are introduced to them before they fully understand how they operate and the proper way to use them. We observe our parents and other adults effortlessly swipe a thin plastic card and receive various items in return. For those who haven't been initiated, this may seem like some form of sorcery where something is obtained without exchanging money. There is a reason credit card companies target college students.

This type of magical thinking can carry over into adulthood. Using a credit card doesn't feel like spending money; instead, it feels more like borrowing money. Although we know we will eventually have to pay the bill, the promise of small minimum payments makes purchases appear to be great deals.

Credit card companies are well aware of this psychological disconnect, and they take advantage of it. As a result, many people find themselves struggling with overwhelming credit card debt. However, by being informed about how credit cards function before utilizing them, we can turn them into useful tools that help improve our financial situation rather than causing harm.

Real money

It's easy to forget that you're using real money when using a credit card, especially when paying with a phone app or using one-click checkout (both tied to a credit card). Every time you use your credit card, you're essentially borrowing money from the issuer until you reach your credit limit (and sometimes even beyond that). This convenience comes at a cost, and many people don't realize the true cost of these loans until they're faced with overwhelming credit card debt.

The price of convenience

Credit card companies are constantly finding ways to make using their cards more convenient for consumers. Their main objective is to encourage individuals to use credit for all their purchases and only make minimum monthly payments, which ultimately leads to higher profits for the company. They entice customers with rewards programs, but also offer the option of minimum payments—which may seem like a manageable monthly expense but can lead to long-term debt. Credit card companies thrive on late payments and penalties, as these mean increased interest rates and more money in their pockets.

One of the main reasons people prefer using credit cards over other payment methods is its simplicity. It eliminates the need to carry cash, allows for larger purchases than one's wallet may hold, and offers the flexibility of paying later. However, there are instances where using a credit card may be the only option, such as booking a hotel room or renting a car. Additionally, credit cards offer added security, as they can easily be cancelled if lost or stolen—compared to cash, which cannot be retrieved once lost.

Credit card companies entice us with bonuses like cashback rewards and points for travel in order to get us to use their services. While they may earn a small profit from each transaction, they also have another motive: They know that many individuals intend to pay off their balances in full but end up falling behind. Maybe they think they'll pay it all off next month, but when the bill arrives, they don't have enough money or they don't want to see such a large sum leaving their account at once—so they just make the minimum payment.

This behavior can easily become a habit, leading individuals down a slippery slope of overspending and only paying the minimum amount due each month. Eventually, this can result in overwhelming debt that seemingly appears out of nowhere. Credit card companies bank on this happening; their goal is for individuals to overspend and carry a balance, as paying off a credit card solely through minimum payments is challenging, expensive, and time-consuming due to compounding interest rates.

Compound interest is good, right?

Compound interest is a powerful tool that can work for or against you, much like credit. It has the amazing ability to grow your investments exponentially by adding earned interest back into the principal amount. "Interest on interest" is the key concept behind compound interest's strength. Albert Einstein famously said, "Compound interest is the eighth wonder of the world. He who understands it, earns it; he who doesn't, pays it." This quote emphasizes the power of compound interest in financial growth and the importance of understanding how it works to benefit from it. Those who grasp the concept can leverage it to build wealth, while those who do not may find themselves burdened by debt due to high-interest loans and credit obligations. (62)

The rule of 72

You may have heard of the "rule of 72"; if not, here is how it works and why it's useful. The rule of 72 is a simple mathematical formula used in finance to estimate how long it will take for an investment to double in value, given a fixed annual rate of return.

If you divide 72 by the annual rate of return on your investment, that's how many years it will take for your money to double. For example, if your investment has a 10% annual rate of return, it will take approximately 7.2 years for your money to double. It's a simple rule— not as precise as detailed financial calculations, but it provides a reasonably accurate estimate, especially at low interest rates.

There are two things the rule of 72 can tell you with reasonable accuracy: how many years it will take to double your money, and what kind of return you will need to double your money in a fixed period of time.

Because you know how long it will take to double your money, it's also easy to figure out how long it would take to quadruple your money. For example, if you can double your money in seven years, you can quadruple it in 14 years by allowing the interest to compound.

Again, it's a simple tool that can give an estimate and shows the power of compounding: interest growing on top of interest.

The rule of 72 working against you

However, a negative effect can occur with credit card debt. When you don't pay off your credit card balance in full, interest is charged on the unpaid amount. This interest is then added to your balance, meaning you'll pay interest on the interest in the next billing cycle. This compounding effect can cause your debt to grow just as rapidly over time. Just as your investments double in 7.2 years at a 10% annual rate of return, the amount you owe will also double in 7.2 years at an annual interest rate of 10%. This is assuming you can find a credit card that only charges 10%!

Let's say you have a balance of $5,000. If your credit card charges 20%, using the rule of 72 we can estimate how long it will take for your credit card debt to double:

72/20 = 3.6 years

So, at a 20% annual interest rate, your credit card debt would approximately double in about 3.6 years if you made no payments and allowed the interest to compound!

In only 3.6 years you would have a new debt balance of $10,000.

However, it's important to note a few key points:

- This is an estimate. The rule of 72 is most accurate for interest rates between 6% and 10%, so at 20% it's a bit less precise.

- Credit card interest usually compounds daily, not annually, which can make the debt grow even faster than this estimate suggests.

- This assumes you're not making any payments at all. Even minimum payments would slow the growth of the debt.

- Credit card debt can spiral out of control quickly due to high interest rates. A balance that doubles in less than four years demonstrates why it's crucial to pay more than the minimum payment and work toward paying off credit card debt as quickly as possible.

- The actual time for your debt to double could be shorter if you continue to use the card and add to the balance.

To avoid this rapid debt growth, it's best to pay off credit card balances in full each month. If that's not possible, paying more than the minimum and avoiding new charges can help slow the growth of the debt and stop compounding interest working against you.

Credit card usage: benefits and drawbacks

When used wisely, credit cards offer a host of benefits:

- **Short-term, interest-free loans:** If you pay off your credit card balance in full every month, you can enjoy an interest-free grace period on your purchases. This can help you manage your cash flow.

- **Rewards:** Many credit cards offer cash-back rewards or other incentives for using the card. This can help you earn extra income on your spending.

- **Consumer protections:** Credit cards often come with various consumer protections, such as fraud protection, purchase protection, extended warranties, or travel insurance. These can help you avoid losses or expenses in case of theft, damage, or disputes.

- **Credit score planning:** Credit cards can help you build and maintain a good credit score, which can affect your ability to get approved for other loans or financial products. A good credit score depends on factors such as paying on time and keeping a low debt-to-credit ratio (the percentage of available credit). A higher credit score can help you qualify for lower interest rates and save money on other debts.

But there are drawbacks as well.

- **High interest rates:** If you don't pay off your credit card balance in full every month, you will incur interest charges that can be very high compared to other forms of debt. This can increase your debt burden.

- **Fees and penalties:** Credit cards may charge fees and penalties for various reasons, such as late payments, exceeding the credit limit, balance transfers, cash advances, or foreign transactions.

- **Debt accumulation:** Credit cards may tempt you to overspend. This can lead to debt accumulation, which can affect your financial plan and goals. You may even struggle to keep track of your spending and payments across multiple cards.

- **Credit score damage:** Credit cards can also hurt your credit score if you misuse them or fail to manage them properly. For example, missing payments, maxing out cards, or applying for too many cards can lower your credit score and make it harder for you to get approved for other loans or financial products. Even canceling an approved credit card can lower your score.

Credit cards are inherently neither good nor bad. They serve as financial tools that can be beneficial or harmful, depending on how you use them. Buyer beware.

Building credit comes first

Most people glance at their credit report without truly looking at it, not recognizing the importance of the numbers and information listed. They only think about it when they're in the process of making a big purchase, like a house, or when they're rejected for credit. **It would be an error** to think that credit reputation is only relevant when borrowing money, as it has become a crucial aspect of life with far-reaching effects.

When it comes to managing your finances, your credit score is a looming number that affects every decision you make. It can determine the type of car you can afford, the amount you can borrow for a home, and even the job opportunities that may be available to you. Despite the constantly changing landscape of personal finance, one thing remains constant: the significance of maintaining a strong credit score. Your credit rating plays a crucial role in your overall financial health. To truly grasp why having good credit is crucial, here are a few examples of how it can help you reach your financial goals.

Access to affordable credit

Having a good credit score has numerous benefits, including access to affordable credit options. Lenders use your credit score as a measure of risk when deciding whether to lend to you. With a high credit score, you demonstrate responsible financial behavior and are more likely to be approved for loans and credit cards with better terms and lower interest rates. This can save you money in the long run, giving you more financial flexibility for goals such as buying a house, financing education, or starting a business.

Easier approval for rental properties

For individuals who are not yet prepared to make the commitment of purchasing a home, renting is often the preferred housing option. However, your credit score still remains a factor. Landlords and property management companies commonly review credit reports when evaluating potential tenants. A solid credit history can be the deciding factor between obtaining your desired rental property or facing rejection.

Enhanced job prospects

Surprisingly, your credit score may have an impact on your professional life. Employers, particularly in the finance industry, may consider reviewing credit reports during their hiring process. Although this practice is limited by specific rules and regulations, having a strong credit history can demonstrate financial reliability and steadiness, potentially increasing the likelihood of securing a job.

Lower insurance premiums

Your credit score can have an effect on the price of insurance as well. Insurance companies commonly use credit-based insurance scores to calculate premiums for auto and homeowners insurance. Generally, individuals with higher credit scores will receive lower insurance premiums, resulting in potential long-term savings.

Improved financial security

Having good credit goes beyond just being able to borrow money and save for the future; it also provides a sense of financial stability. A solid credit record can serve as a safety net in times of need. With a strong credit score, you are more likely to qualify for a personal loan or credit card with beneficial conditions, which can come in handy for unexpected costs like medical bills or emergency home repairs.

Building wealth and achieving long-term goals

Establishing a good credit score is a crucial step in achieving long-term financial success and building wealth. It provides access to investment opportunities, such as buying income-generating properties or other investments. A strong credit score also opens doors to affordable credit options and better financial prospects, allowing you to grow your wealth over time.

The significance of building good credit cannot be overstated. It impacts every aspect of your financial life and can determine the difference between financial stability and hardship. By practicing responsible financial habits, such as paying bills on time and managing debt wisely, you can create and maintain a solid credit history that will help you reach your financial goals and secure your future. Remember, it's not just about having good credit; it's about building a brighter financial future for yourself and your loved ones.

However, keep in mind that building good credit takes patience and consistent responsible financial behavior. This includes making timely payments, keeping your credit usage low, and managing various types of credit accounts wisely. With dedication and discipline, you can achieve a strong credit score that will benefit you for years to come.

Establishing credit when you don't have any?

Here are some effective ways to establish credit when you don't have any credit history:

- **Become an authorized user on someone else's credit card:** Ask a family member or trusted friend with good credit to add you as an authorized user on their credit card account. Their positive payment history will be reported on your credit file, helping you build credit.

- **Apply for a secured credit card:** These cards require a cash deposit that serves as collateral and typically have lower credit requirements. Use the card responsibly and make on-time payments to build credit.

- **Use Experian Boost or similar services to add utility, rent, and other payments to your credit report.**

- **Consider a secured loan from a credit union:** Some credit unions offer small secured loans to help members establish credit.

- **Get a co-signer for a loan or credit card:** A co-signer with good credit can help you qualify.

- **Open a checking/savings account and manage it responsibly:** While this doesn't directly build credit, it can help you qualify for credit products from that bank in the future.

Remember to always make payments on time, keep credit utilization low, and be patient—building credit takes time. Regularly monitor your credit report to track your progress and ensure accuracy.

Next, let's discuss strategies for paying off debt

CHAPTER 13

HOW TO PAY OFF DEBT

Stress

The realization struck me like a punch to the gut. I had been avoiding checking my credit card balance for weeks, knowing that it wouldn't be pretty, but the sheer size of the number staring back at me now was staggering.

It wasn't just a few hundred dollars over my limit, or even a couple thousand. It was a five-digit number that made my head spin and my heart race. How had I let it get this bad? I had always been careful with my spending, keeping a close eye on my budget and paying off my credit card bill in full each month.

But then life happened—unexpected expenses and emergencies that drained my savings and forced me to rely on my credit card more and more. And somewhere along the way, I stopped keeping track. I stopped being responsible.

I stared at the number, trying to make sense of it. It was almost as if it had taken on a life of its own, growing and multiplying without my knowledge. How had I not seen it sooner? How had I let it get so out of control?

The weight of my financial burden loomed over me, threatening to crush me under its heavy weight. I knew I needed to face it, to come up with a plan to pay it off and regain control of my finances. But in that moment, all I could do was stare at the number and wonder how I had let it escalate to this point.

Debt stacking method

How do you eat an elephant? One bite at a time.

The same is true for paying off debt. You tackle it one bite at a time, in small chunks. I recommend a method called **"debt stacking."** By looking at interest rates and the amount of debt, "debt stacking" lays out a system for prioritizing your debt repayment.

Step 1: List all your debt, including the interest rate, remaining payments, and minimum payment.

It might look a little overwhelming, but stick with me. You can do this. An Excel spreadsheet works great for this, or you can use a whiteboard.

Step 2: Budget how much money you can contribute to your debt each month.

Think of your debt payment as one lump sum. **Within your Pay Yourself First setup, your debt payment should come from your checking account.**

Step 3: Break out the lump sum into payments for each debt, and start paying them down.

Use the spreadsheet to separate the payment into each consumer debt. Prioritize the debt with the highest interest rate: Focus the bulk of the debt payment onto that debt while ensuring you make at least the minimum payment against all your remaining debts.

Step 4: Once you've paid off the first debt you prioritized, roll that payment onto the next highest interest rate.

The next debt will be eliminated faster because you'll be making a larger monthly payment against it. These extra dollars help reduce the effect of compound interest working against you.

Step 5: Repeat until you're debt free!

It's important to note that debt stacking works best when you avoid accruing new debts during the repayment process. (63)

The debt snowball method

While debt stacking can be mathematically more efficient, there is another approach that's also very effective, called the debt snowball method, where you pay off the smallest debt first while making minimum payments on all other debts. Once you've paid off the smallest debt in full, you move on to the next smallest, and so on.

The debt snowball method contrasts with the debt stacking method, which prioritizes paying off debts with the highest interest rates first. The choice between these methods often depends on personal preference and what keeps an individual motivated to continue paying off debt.

The debt snowball method can have a significant positive impact on mental motivation compared to other debt repayment strategies. Here are some key ways it affects motivation: (63)

- **Quick wins:** By focusing on paying off the smallest debts first, the debt snowball method allows you to achieve "quick wins" early in the process. Paying off an entire debt, even if it's small, provides a sense of accomplishment and progress.

- **Psychological boost:** Seeing debts disappear one by one can increase your motivation to continue paying off debt. Even paying off a small balance can boost your confidence and create momentum.

- **Simplification:** As you pay off each debt, you have fewer monthly payments to manage. This simplification can reduce stress and make the overall debt burden feel more manageable.

- **Visible progress:** The debt snowball method provides clear, tangible progress as you eliminate debts one by one. This visibility can be more motivating than slowly chipping away at larger balances.

- **Habit formation:** This method helps build positive financial habits and discipline as you consistently allocate extra funds to debt repayment.

- **Reduced overwhelm:** By focusing on one debt at a time, the snowball method can help reduce the feeling of being overwhelmed by multiple debts.

- **Dopamine effect:** Achieving milestones (paying off individual debts) triggers dopamine release in the brain, providing a reward sensation that motivates continued effort.

Tonya and I loved the debt snowball method and used a white-board to track our debt. There was great satisfaction in literally wiping out each debt on the dry eraser board. Boom! Another one down. I would also suggest writing a reward at the end of each killed debt. It doesn't have to be big, but you should celebrate the small victories. Make it as fun as possible. Well, as fun as paying off debt can be... And when you buy your reward, use cash!

Debt stacking versus debt snowball

While other methods, like debt stacking or the debt avalanche (focusing on debts with the highest interest rates first), may save more money mathematically, research has shown that the psychological benefits of the debt snowball method often lead to better adherence and success rates for many people.

Choosing the Right Method

The best method depends on your personal circumstances and psychological factors:

- If you're motivated by efficiency and saving money, the debt stacking method may be preferable.

- If you need psychological wins to stay motivated, the debt snowball method might work better for you.

- Some people opt for a hybrid approach, combining elements of both methods.

- Consider your debt amounts, interest rates, and personal motivation when deciding.

The motivational aspect can be particularly helpful for those who've struggled with debt repayment in the past or feel over-whelmed by their debt load. However, it's important to note that the best method depends on individual circumstances and preferences. Some people may find other strategies more motivating or effective for their specific situation.

Remember, the most effective debt repayment strategy is the one you can stick to consistently. All methods require discipline and commitment to extra payments beyond the minimum amount due. (63)

Should you pay off your mortgage early?

Is it wise to pay off your mortgage early? This seemingly simple question can spark heated debates among different groups. While some homeowners have a relatively low mortgage interest rate, others may wonder if investing that extra money would yield better returns. Owning a home is a major accomplishment, but the journey to pay off the mortgage can feel like an endless marathon. The idea of paying it off early may be tempting, but is it a smart financial decision for you? While it may not be the most exciting investment strategy, paying off your mortgage has numerous benefits that can greatly impact your financial stability, overall quality of life, and generosity toward others.

Benefits of paying off your montage early

Save money by reducing interest payments

The primary benefit of paying off your mortgage early is the potential savings on interest payments. The longer you have a mortgage, the more interest you'll end up paying. Paying off your mortgage early can significantly reduce the total amount of interest you pay over the life of the loan.

For example, let's say you have a 30-year fixed-rate mortgage for $200,000 with an interest rate of 4%. If you make the minimum monthly payments, you'll end up paying a total of $143,739 in interest over 30 years. However, if you were to pay an extra $100 each month toward your principal balance, you could save over $24,000 in interest and pay off your mortgage 4 years and 11 months earlier.

Additionally, by reducing your overall debt through early repayment of your mortgage, you can improve your credit score. A lower debt-to-income ratio and less outstanding debt can positively affect your credit score and open up opportunities for better financing options in the future.

Peace of mind

Another key benefit to paying off your mortgage early is the peace of mind it can bring. Having a large amount of debt hanging over your head can be stressful and limit financial freedom. By eliminating this burden, you can feel more financially secure and have greater control over your financial choices. This sense of security and peace of mind can also have positive effects on other areas of life, such as relationships and overall well-being.

Increased cash flow

As soon as your mortgage is paid off, the amount you spend on housing each month will decrease significantly. Without the weight of paying off a mortgage, you will have more money available to you. You can use this additional cash to increase your charitable giving, invest in different assets, or simply enhance your overall well-being.

One of the biggest burdens of retirement is eliminated

Retirement is a highly anticipated stage of life, but it also brings financial challenges. Housing expenses, such as mortgage payments, can be a major source of stress for retirees. Research shows that housing costs can consume up to one-third of a retiree's income. By paying off your mortgage before retiring, you free yourself from this significant financial burden and open up the opportunity for your retirement years to be some of the most fulfilling and impactful years of your life, dedicated to advancing good causes and making a positive impact in the world.

Opportunity for generosity

Paying off your mortgage early also frees up additional funds that would otherwise go toward monthly payments. This extra money can be used to invest or save for other goals such as retirement or college tuition. However, it also presents an opportunity to be more generous toward others. Whether it's supporting family members or giving back to causes that are important to you, having financial stability and flexibility allows for greater acts of generosity.

Disadvantages of paying off your mortgage early

While paying off your mortgage loan early has numerous advantages, it's not a flawless strategy. There are also drawbacks that must be carefully considered before making any decisions.

Lost investment opportunities

While paying off your mortgage early can reduce the amount of interest you pay, investing that money instead may provide a greater return over time. This is due to the concept of opportunity cost: the funds used to pay off your mortgage could potentially earn a higher return if invested in other opportunities.

Reduced liquidity

Paying off your mortgage in advance means that most of your money is tied up in your home, which could limit your flexibility when it comes to other financial needs or potential investments. Using your savings or allocating a large amount of cash toward paying off your mortgage may leave you with minimal funds for unexpected expenses. While selling your house is an option, it's not a quick and easy solution and may take time to generate the necessary funds. It's always recommended to have a substantial emergency fund available in case of any unforeseen circumstances.

Saving money vs. paying off debt

One of the most common financial struggles for many of us is finding the right balance between saving money and paying off debt. While the answer depends on individual circumstances, it's important to prioritize both.

Eliminating high-interest debt in a timely manner can decrease the overall amount of interest paid and free up funds in your budget for other expenses. However, not having enough savings for emergencies can lead to accumulating more credit card debt when unexpected costs arise.

It may feel impossible to save money while trying to pay off debt, but striking a balance between the two is crucial for long-term financial management. It doesn't have to be an all-or-nothing approach; you can and should work toward both goals. Building an emergency fund, even if it starts small and grows slowly, can prevent added stress when unexpected situations occur.

When to make saving a priority

Here are some valid reasons for putting more of a focus on saving money than reducing debt.

Emergency fund

Having a solid emergency fund is crucial. It acts as a financial cushion, providing you with a safety net in case of any unforeseen expenses. Whether it's a small home repair or the loss of a job, this fund can help you overcome any unexpected hurdles. The general guideline is to save enough money to cover three to six months worth of expenses in your emergency fund.

Retirement savings

Don't wait until you've paid off all of your debt to start saving for retirement. By starting early, you can take advantage of compound interest and grow your nest egg faster. Waiting too long will result in a significant decrease in your overall retirement savings. If your job offers a 401(k)-match program, make sure to contribute enough to receive the full amount. This could be extra money that you're missing out on if you don't take advantage of it. Don't let insufficient retirement funds hold you back from financial stability.

Not all debt is bad

Not all debts are harmful; in fact, some can have a positive impact on your overall financial health. For example, student loans can fund your education and open better job opportunities with higher earning potential. Taking out a mortgage can lead to owning a valuable property that appreciates in value, leading to potential profits. Simply put, having some debt may not always be a negative aspect of your financial portfolio.

How to balance saving and paying off debt

Get organized

As mentioned before, it's important to get organized with your debts. Make a list of all your outstanding balances, along with the interest rate and minimum payment for each one. This will help you see exactly how much debt you have and how much it's costing you in the long run.

Revisit your budget

Start by calculating your monthly take-home pay, then factor in all of your monthly expenses. This includes necessary bills, any debts you're paying off each month, and any discretionary spending like shopping or entertainment. If your expenses exceed your income, you'll need to make adjustments to reduce your spending.

Track your spending

Take a moment to review your bank and credit card statements from the past few months. This will help you identify any patterns in your spending habits. You may also come across unnecessary expenses, such as memberships or subscriptions that you aren't utilizing and can cut out.

Determine how much extra income you have each month

A good rule to follow is setting aside 20% of your take-home pay for financial goals. This amount can be divided between saving and paying off debt. If 20% seems like too much, start with a smaller percentage and save whatever you can afford.

Set a savings goal

Your savings goal will be unique to you, so start by assessing your current emergency fund. If you don't have one yet, don't worry—the best time to start saving is always now. Instead of aiming for three months worth of expenses right away, start with a more manageable goal, like building a mini emergency fund of $1,000.

Next, consider when you want to reach this goal. For instance, if you save $100 each month, you'll hit $1,000 in 10 months. Your monthly budget will play a role in determining your timeline. If you have $500 per month to allocate toward savings and debt, that will impact how quickly you can reach your goal. You might divide it up like this:

- $100 in your emergency fund
- $300 toward debt
- $100 in a retirement account

Choose a debt repayment strategy

Consider implementing either the debt snowball or debt stacking method, both of which were previously discussed. Another option is debt consolidation, which entails taking out a loan with a lower interest rate than your current debts and using it to pay all of your off. This would leave you with one balance and a single monthly payment. Alternatively, you could utilize a credit card with a 0% introductory interest rate for balance transfers.

Contribute enough to your 401(k) to get an employer match

Many employers offer to match their employees' contributions to their 401(k) plans or other retirement plans, which can be a great benefit. If this applies to you, it's smart to contribute enough to take advantage of that match. Essentially, it's free money being added to your retirement savings. Usually, employers will match between 3% and 5% of an employee's pay. And with the power of compound interest, that extra money could grow significantly over time. This is an important factor to consider when deciding how much to save every month, but it may require a balancing act to find the right amount.

The bottom line

It's not always necessary to decide between paying off debt and building your savings. It is possible to achieve both goals and find a balance that fits your budget. Striking the right balance between debt repayment and saving is crucial for achieving financial stability. With a well-planned budget and specific targets, you can effectively manage your finances and prepare for any potential financial obstacles. Regularly reviewing and modifying your plan as needed is also essential. It's never too late to start working toward both saving and paying off debt. The key is to maintain consistency.

CHAPTER 14

PUTTING IT ALL TOGETHER

Money is unique in that it affects our daily lives in so many ways—whether we're using it, thinking about it, spending it, saving it, or worrying about it. The issue isn't money itself; it's the emotions that arise because of money. No wonder it's difficult to discuss with your spouse—or anyone else for that matter.

Avoiding discussions about finances in order to prevent tension only results in more tension in the long run. Surprisingly, I have seen that the ability to communicate effectively about money, even if it feels uncomfortable and awkward, is more crucial than having a large financial cushion. In fact, couples with ample financial resources but poor communication skills are more likely to experience damaging tensions due to money-related concerns—such as anxiety, stress, avoidance, and feeling neglected—compared to those with less wealth but open channels of communication.

In other words, the misconception that wealth solves all problems is false. It's commonly assumed that couples with more money have an easier time because they don't have to argue over limited resources. However, this is often not the case. Money goes beyond just numbers— otherwise, wealthy couples wouldn't argue about it. It evokes strong emotions and insecurities within us all. Our thoughts and fears can either lead to disagreements or foster deeper connections between us.

As a financial advisor, one of my greatest obstacles is helping couples establish open and honest communication about their finances. This is a crucial first step before we can even begin discussing things like budgeting, paying off debts, saving for retirement, or investing. Communication must come first before we can create a solid financial plan together.

Why is it so difficult for couples to communicate?

Why is it such a struggle for couples to communicate about money? Despite their attempts, men and women often find themselves at odds when discussing finances. Money is a complex and powerful topic, which may contribute to the difficulty in truly understanding or resolving issues surrounding it. It's possible that this challenge arises from the unique backgrounds and fears held by each of us.

Men often fear not being able to provide for their families or losing financial stability, creating a significant pressure on them as the primary providers. This fear can make them reluctant to talk about money to avoid conflicts or feelings of inadequacy. On the other hand, women typically take on the role of caregivers within the family unit and place greater emphasis on maintaining strong relationships and a sense of unity among their loved ones. For them, financial stability is a long-term concern, and they may worry about the possibility of being financially dependent in the future. This fear can cause them to be more cautious with their money and avoid taking any significant financial risks. Of course, these are broad statements, and responsibilities in a partnership may vary significantly. The key is recognizing the differing perspectives and understanding how they may impact communication and decision-making when it comes to finances.

Conflicting fears surrounding money often lead to communication breakdowns and misunderstandings between couples. Each person is so preoccupied with their own worries that they have difficulty empathizing with their partner's point of view. Unfortunately, in an ironic twist, one person's attempts to protect themselves or alleviate their fears may actually trigger the other person's fears, albeit unintentionally.

The weight of societal expectations is heavy on both genders when it comes to money. For men, traditional gender roles assign them the role of being the primary provider, the one responsible for putting food on the table and a roof over their family's heads. This pressure can be crushing, especially in a world where job security is uncertain and the cost of living is constantly rising. Men are expected to be strong, both physically and financially, and any perceived failure in this regard could be viewed as weakness or inadequacy. They often feel the need to project success and hide any financial struggles, leading to a culture of toxic masculinity.

On the other hand, women are often discouraged from being involved in managing money. They are expected to focus on the domestic sphere and leave the financial decisions to their husbands. This lack of involvement could result in dire consequences if their partner were to pass away, leaving them suddenly responsible for their finances without any prior knowledge or experience.

Society's rigid expectations often hinder both genders from making sound financial choices, and it's time for a change. Both men and women should feel empowered to take control of their finances and make informed decisions, without the fear of judgment or societal backlash. Acknowledging these dynamics allows partners to have more effective discussions about money and work together toward a financially stable future. Recognizing each other's unique pressures and sources of stress can enhance communication and strengthen the bond between partners.

Open and honest

Having open and honest conversations is essential for building a strong financial foundation as a couple. Overcoming obstacles through transparent communication about money is crucial. It's important to recognize the differences in our money mindsets as a starting point for productive financial discussions. Each of us may have unique attitudes and behaviors toward money, shaped by our upbringing, experiences, and culture. Understanding these varying mindsets, whether it's a scarcity or abundance mentality, can help us compromise on financial decisions together—because, let's face it, no one wants to end up in a budget battle over who spent more on takeout this month!

Talking about power dynamics is also key, since finances can often be linked to control and dominance in relationships. Addressing how we manage finances, involve each other in decision-making, and balance power in financial matters can lead to more open conversations about money. Improving communication about finances means approaching discussions with empathy toward one another. Putting yourself in your partner's shoes and considering their perspective can prevent defensiveness or dismissing their views. Regular check-ins on budgets, upcoming expenses, and income changes can prevent surprises, while active listening ensures both partners feel heard and understood during money talks.

Shifting our focus from individual desires to shared goals, like saving for retirement or buying a house together, can align us toward a common purpose when managing our finances as a couple. By working together toward these shared objectives, we can strengthen our financial partnership and build a more secure future together.

Dealing with conflicts and differences in values

In every relationship, it's essential to acknowledge and respect the values of both individuals, even if they're not entirely in sync—or may never be so. This is a crucial component of creating a robust and positive connection: understanding your partner's values and where they find value is key.

The first step in dealing with differences in values is recognizing that they exist. This means being aware of your own values and understanding that your partner may have different ones. It's also important to be open-minded and respectful of each other's values, even if you don't agree with them. Instead of getting defensive or attacking the other person's beliefs, try to engage in a calm and understanding conversation. Listen actively to each other's perspectives and try to find common ground.

For instance, I prefer the convenience and time-saving aspect of shopping at Publix, while my partner Tonya prioritizes affordability and opts for Walmart or Aldi. Additionally, one person may indulge in a daily Starbucks coffee as part of their daily routine, whereas the other may choose to invest in a cappuccino maker to save money and time in the long run.

Compromise is essential in any relationship where there are conflicting values. This doesn't mean giving up on your own values but rather finding a middle ground that works for both individuals.

It's also important to understand that some differences in values may never be resolved, nor do they necessarily need to be. Some things may be non-negotiable for one person while the other can compromise on them. In these situations, it's crucial to accept and respect each other's individuality.

It's also essential to recognize when a conflict or difference in values may stem from deeper issues, such as past experiences or personal beliefs. In these cases, it may be helpful to seek outside help from a therapist or counselor who can facilitate discussions and provide guidance on how to navigate these sensitive topics.

Conflicts and differences in values are natural occurrences in relationships. By acknowledging their existence, communicating effectively, compromising, accepting each other's individuality, and seeking outside help when needed, you can strengthen your connection and find ways to coexist despite these differences.

It's worth the effort!

My desire is for this book to have pushed you and your partner to grow. I hope it has sparked conversations about understanding each other on a deeper level, even in a relationship that has many wonderful qualities. Our attitudes toward money reveal our past influences and lessons about it, as well as our fears and desires—even if they're not based in reality.

When a relationship begins, it's natural to inquire about each other's upbringing and family dynamics. It can be helpful to understand your partner's relationships with their parents, siblings, and past romantic partners in order to grasp their character and how past events have influenced them leading up to the present moment. Additionally, gaining insight into their attitudes toward money is crucial.

If you haven't taken the time to really delve into this aspect of your partner, now is the perfect opportunity. It may be uncomfortable at first, but it's necessary in order to address your own issues and gain a deeper understanding of your partner. By truly understanding each other, your relationship will thrive. Don't shy away from discussing financial matters; once you start, you'll see how much it strengthens your bond.

What really matters

Everyone's financial journey is different; maybe you've always had a positive relationship with money and never faced any challenges or difficulties, effectively communicating about it from the start. Or maybe money is just one source of stress in your marriage, among others. No matter what your circumstances, taking the time to understand how you and your partner handle money will greatly benefit your relationship.

After all, as I mentioned before, our approach to money offers a glimpse into our inner thoughts and emotions. With some effort, you can overcome any hesitation about discussing financial matters and instead focus on developing positive habits that will truly improve your marriage. And remember, this process doesn't have to be difficult, especially if you let go of the false belief that more money will solve all of your problems. Rather, there are several key habits that can truly bring about positive change in every aspect of your life.

Believe your spouse cares

In this book, I have explored how our thoughts about money can be shaped by our individual differences. Men and women, in particular, may have conflicting views on the subject. However, it's vital to remember that both partners still care for each other. It's crucial to trust and believe that your partner has good intentions and cares for you, even if their opinions on money may differ from yours. Just because they may not agree with how you handle finances doesn't mean they do not care for you.

Understanding this can help you overcome conflicts or disagreements about money in your relationship. Instead of assuming the worst about your partner's intentions, choose to trust that they care for you and want what's best for both of you.

Working together

One way to build trust and strengthen your relationship when it comes to finances is by working together as a team. Instead of keeping financial matters separate, make an effort to involve each other in decisions and be transparent about your spending habits. This not only shows trust in your partner but also creates a sense of unity in managing your finances. By working together, you can come up with a budget or financial plan that takes into account both of your perspectives and goals.

Compromise is key

In any relationship, compromise is crucial for maintaining harmony. This is especially true when it comes to finances, where two individuals with different attitudes toward money must come together.

When faced with conflicting views on how money should be spent or saved, try to find a middle ground that satisfies both partners. For example, if one partner likes to splurge on vacations while the other prefers saving for retirement, consider compromising by taking budget-friendly trips or finding ways to save while still enjoying a vacation.

Live in hope

Living in hope is like standing on the edge of a cliff, looking out at a vast and endless horizon. The future is uncertain, but the vibrant colors of the sunset paint the sky with optimism and possibility. This is an essential habit to cultivate when it comes to our relationship with money. It involves adopting a positive mindset and focusing on the potential for growth and abundance in all areas of our lives.

Set realistic goals

Having hope means believing that things can get better, but it also requires taking action toward achieving those improvements. Setting realistic financial goals is crucial in this process.

Instead of chasing after unrealistic dreams or comparing ourselves to others, we should focus on setting achievable goals that align with our values and priorities. This could include paying off debt, saving for a down payment on a house, or investing for retirement. By breaking down these goals into manageable steps and creating a plan to reach them, we can build hope and motivation to work toward them.

Choose gratitude

In the pursuit of financial success, it's easy to fall into a mindset of always wanting more. However, this constant desire for more can lead us to overlook what we already have. Cultivating gratitude helps us shift our focus from what we lack to what we are fortunate enough to possess.

Take some time each day to reflect on what you're grateful for regarding your relationships and your finances— whether it's having a stable job, being able to pay bills on time, or having a supportive partner. This practice can foster feelings of contentment and hopefulness, rather than constantly feeling like there's never enough.

You might still think your significant other is crazy, but my aim is for both of you to gain a deeper understanding of each other.

You can do this

You have the ability to improve your understanding of both your partner's intentions and your own beliefs and values when it comes to managing money. With this information, you can enhance your communication skills and effectively manage your finances, setting yourself on the path toward financial security. I want to reassure you that you're capable of achieving this and to offer my support along the way.

Your ability to perceive your partner's intentions when it comes to financial management is not just a skill but an art, and one that can be honed and improved over time. It's like learning a new language, a dance of numbers and shared goals. With every conversation, every transaction, you start to understand their patterns, their habits, their silent hopes and fears about money.

Imagine each decision they make as a stroke on a canvas— not random or arbitrary, but revealing a deeper picture of their financial philosophy. The choice to save may reflect a fear of uncertainty, while the decision to splurge could hint at a desire for instant gratification. As you piece these clues together, you begin to see the intricate tapestry of their financial mindset.

And once you've cracked this code, once you've unlocked the door into their financial psyche, how then do you respond? You respond by enhancing your communication skills. By learning to speak their language. By understanding not just what they're saying, but why they're saying it. The goal is not just to be heard, but to be understood. To create a space where both of you can talk openly about money without fear or judgment.

With these tools in your arsenal, you can then navigate the complex world of financial management with greater ease. Every decision you make, every plan you execute will bring you one step closer to this goal.

I believe in your capability to master this art, to turn this challenge into an opportunity for growth. And as you embark on this journey, remember that every step you take, every obstacle you overcome is a testament to your resilience and determination. It's not just about managing money; it's about creating a future that aligns with both your dreams and your realities.

NOTES

Chapter 1

1. CFP Board, Understanding the clients personal and financial circumstances, Jan, 2019, Understanding the Client's Personal and Financial Circumstances | CFP Board

2. https://www.letsmakeaplan.org/

Chapter 2

3. "Most Americans Are significantly stressed about money-here's how it varies by demographic". Sheiresa McRae Ngo, Bankrate, June 03, 2024, Money And Financial Stress Statistics | Bankrate

4. "Researcher finds correlation between financial arguments, decreased relationship satisfaction", Sonya Britt, Kansas State University, July 12, 2013 Researcher finds correlation between financial arguments, decreased relationship satisfaction | Kansas State University | News and Communications Services (k-state.edu)

5. "Money, Marriage, and Communication", Ramsey, September 27, 2021, Money, Marriage, and Communication - Ramsey (ramseysolutions.com)

6. "The Importance of Money Conversations", Kathy Longo. LinkedIn, September 5, 2018, https://www.linkedin.com/in/kathleenlongo?trk=article-ssr-frontend-pulse_publisher-author-card

7. "Why financial literacy is essential in relationships" Tamara Miller-Falls, February 21, 2023, Cache Flo, https://www.cacheflo.co/posts/why-financial-literacy-is-essential-in-relationships

8. "The Influence of Parental Income on Children's Outcomes", Susan E. Mayer, Knowledge Management Group, Ministry of Social Development, Te Manatu Whakahiato Ora, 2002 influence-of-parental-income.pdf (msd.govt.nz)

Chapter 3

9. "Men & Money: Facing The Pressure To Provide", Dr. April Brewer, Better help, March 23, 2024, Men & Money: Facing The Pressure To Financially Provide | BetterHelp

10. "Psychological Well-Being in Retirement: The Effects of Personal and Gendered Contextual Resources", J Occup Health Psychol. April 16, 2011, Psychological Well-Being in Retirement: The Effects of Personal and Gendered Contextual Resources - PMC (nih.gov)

11. "The science behind financial stress and the gender divide", N26, March 7, 2021 The science behind financial stress and the gender divide (n26.com)

12. "Survey: 47% of Americans say money is negatively impacting their mental health", Lane Gillespie, Bankrate, May 9, 2024 https://www.bankrate.com/loans/personal-loans/money-and-mental-health-survey/

Chapter 4

13. "How couples answer one question shows whether they communicate well about money, Cornell research finds", Lorie Konish, CNBC, June 24, 2024, Why couples avoid talking about financial issues — and how to change (cnbc.com)

Chapter 5

14. "The Psychology of Money: Unraveling Money Beliefs and Mindsets", Averil, Therapy Co., July 14, 2023, The Psychology of Money: Unraveling Money Beliefs and Mindsets (therapyco.co.nz)

15. "9 Signs You Have a Scarcity Money Mindset", Sam Garrison, sidehustles.com, June 29, 2023, 9 Signs You Have a Scarcity Money Mindset & How to Change It (sidehustles.com)

16. "What Is Money Mindset?", Sam Swenson, The Motley Fool, Nov 21, 2023, How to Change Your Money Mindset | The Motley Fool

17. "There are 4 Money Mindsets and whichever one you have will dictate how financially successful you are", Karen Sutton-Johal, LinkedIn, Jan 29, 2021, There are 4 Money Mindsets and whichever one you have will dictate how financially successful you are. (linkedin.com)

18. "How to Shift Your Money Mindset in 5 Easy Steps", Money Mentors, How to Shift Your Money Mindset in 5 Easy Steps (moneymentors.ca)

Chapter 6

19. "Marriage: A Story of Live in 28 Parts' has long-time couples rolling", Annie Reneau, Jan 9, 2021, UPWORTHY, 'Marriage: A Story of Love in 28 Parts' has long-time couples rolling - Upworthy

20. "3 Secrets to a Happy Marriage: Respect, Kindness & Appreciation" Nurturing Marriage, Feb 18, 2016, Values to Live By - NURTURING MARRIAGE®

21. "Masters of Love", Emily Smith, The Atlantic, June 12, 2014, The Secret to Love Is Just Kindness - The Atlantic

22. "6 Steps for Resolving Conflict in Marriage", Dennis Rainey, Family Life, 2002, 6 Steps for Resolving Conflict in Marriage - FamilyLife®

23. "Managing Conflict: Solvable vs. Perpetual Problems", The Gottman Institute, July 26, 2024, "Managing Conflict: Solvable vs. Perpetual Problems"

24. "Resolving Conflict in Marriage", Mike San Martino, Mill Creek Christian Counseling, October 14,2020, Resolving Conflict in Marriage | Mill Creek Christian Counseling

Chapter 7

25. "Cheap Clients" and The Psychology of Small Purchases", Jenika, May 15, 2013, Psychology for photographers, "Cheap Clients" and The Psychology of Small Purchases - Psychology for Photographers and other Creative Professionals

26. "The Psychology of Spending and How to Manage It", Financial Wellness, April 15, 2024, The Psychology of Spending and How to Manage It | St. Mary's Bank (stmarysbank.com)

Chapter 8

27. "A Man's Fear about Being a Man", John Cuddeback, Feb 16, 2022, Life Craft, A Man's Fear about Being a Man - LifeCraft (life-craft.org)

28. "Mend tend to regulate their emotions through actions rather than words", Peter Wright, The Centre For Male Psychology, Men tend to regulate their emotions through actions rather than words — The Centre for Male Psychology

29. "Take Control of Your Relationship By Understanding Men! Part6: Money and Its Importance to Men", Bregg Michaelsen, Gregg Michaelsen Dating & Life Coach, Understand Money and Its Importance to Men | Michaelsen (whoholdsthecardsnow.com)

30. "Women's earning were 83.6 percent of men's in 2023", U.S. Bureau of Labor Statistics, March 12, 2024, Women's earnings were 83.6 percent of men's in 2023 : The Economics Daily: U.S. Bureau of Labor Statistics (bls.gov)

31. "Women and mental health: Psychosocial Perspective", National Library of Medicine, Kalpana Srivastava, June 21, 2012, Women and mental health: Psychosocial perspective - PMC (nih.gov)

32. "Gender Socialization: Examples, Agents & Impact", Simply Psychology, Olivia Guy-Evans, February 13, 2024, Gender Socialization: Examples, Agents & Impact (simplypsychology.org)

33. "Is Retail Therapy for Real?", WebMD, Dan Brennan, MD, September 10, 2021, Retail Therapy: Why Does Shopping Feel Good? (webmd.com)

Chapter 9

34. "The Psychology of Money: Navigating Emotional Hurdles for Wealth Achievement", Chris Hindle, Frazer James, July 2024, The Psychology of Money Navigating Emotional Hurdles for Wealth Achievement (frazer-james.co.uk)

35. "The Psychology of Money: Overcoming Financial Mindset Barriers in your 20s", Saniya V, LinkedIn, May 16,2023, The Psychology of Money: Overcoming Financial Mindset Barriers in Your 20s ☐ (linkedin.com)

36. "The Psychology of Personal Finance", Nextgen, Steven Fox, Feb 2023, The Psychology of Personal Finance - Next Gen Financial Planning

Chapter 10

37. "How To Start An Emergency Savings Fund", CFP Board of Standards, Inc., Troy Jones, March 30, 2022, How to Start an Emergency Savings Fund | CFP - Let's Make a Plan (letsmakeaplan.org)

38. "Retirement Savings and Income Planning", CFP Board of Standards Inc, cfp-board-pkt-learning-objectives---retirement-savings-and-income-planning.pdf

39. "How to Start Saving for College", Big Future, www.bigfuture.collegeboard.org, How to Start Saving for College – BigFuture | College Board

40. "Education Savings", CFP Board of Standards Inc., Education Savings | CFP - Let's Make a Plan (letsmakeaplan.org)

41. "Financial Planning and Application of the Practice Standards for the Financial Planning Process", CFP Board of Standards Inc., January 16, 2020, Frequently Asked Questions about Financial Planning and Application of the Practice Standards for the Financial Planning Process | CFP Board

42. "New Research Shows Significant Gaps Between Advisor, Consumer Views on Money Management", CFP Board of Standards Inc., March 6, 2019, New Research Shows Significant Gaps Between Advisor, Consumer Views on Money Management | CFP Board

43. "Navigating Financial Waters: The Benefits of Working with a Certified Financial Planner(TM)", Payant Wealth Management Group, Tomas Payant, April 26,2024, The Advantages of Working with a Certified Financial Planner (CFP) (payantwealthmanagementgroup.com)

44. "Why Get Certified", CFP Board of Standards Inc., Why Get Certified | CFP Board

45. "What Are the Benefits of Working with a Financial Advisor? – 2021 Study", Smart Asset, Stephanie Horan, July 27, 2023, What Are the Benefits of Working With a Financial Advisor? - 2021 Study - SmartAsset

46. "Benefits of Employing CFP® Professionals", CFP Board of Standards Inc., Benefits of Employing CFP® Professionals | CFP Board

Chapter 11

47. "Center for Microeconomic Data", "Household Debt and Credit Report", Federal Reserve Bank of New York, Q2,2024, Household Debt and Credit Report - FEDERAL RESERVE BANK of NEW YORK (newyorkfed.org)

48. "Average American Household Debt in 2024: Facts and Figures", The Ascent, Jack Caporal, Aug 26, 2024, Average American Household Debt in 2024: Facts and Figures | The Motley Fool

49. "Average American Household Debt in 2024", The Ascent, Jack Caporal, Aug 26, 2024, Average American Credit Card Debt in 2024 | The Motley Fool

50. "Money in Ancient Mesopotamia: Value, Forms, Development", Money in Mesopotamia, Facts and Details, Money in Ancient Mesopotamia: Value, Forms, Development | Middle East And North Africa — Facts and Details

51. "Loan Collateral – Weirdest Things Ever Used", Key Credit Repair, Loan Collateral - Weirdest Things Ever Used (keycreditrepair.com)

52. "Revolving credit", Wikipedia, Revolving credit - Wikipedia

53. "Unsecured Debt", Investopedia, Jason Fernando, February 24, 2021, Unsecured Debt Definition (investopedia.com)

54. "Predatory Lending: How to Avoid, Examples and Protections", Investopedia, Adam Hayes, May 23, 2023, Predatory Lending: How to Avoid, Examples and Protections (investopedia.com)

55. "Predatory Lending", Wikipedia, Predatory lending - Wikipedia

56. "Spotting and Preventing Predatory Lending", My Home by Freddie Mac, May 21, 2024, Spotting and Preventing Predatory Lending - My Home by Freddie Mac

57. "Predatory Lending: How to Avoid, Examples and Protections", Investopedia, Adam Hayes, may 23, 2023, Predatory Lending: How to Avoid, Examples and Protections (investopedia.com)

Chapter 12

58. "Direct Subsidized and Direct Unsubsidized Loans", Federal Student Aid, Subsidized and Unsubsidized Loans | Federal Student Aid

59. "How much can you borrow in student loans?", Hannah Bareham, Bankrate, April 28, 2023, How Much Can You Borrow In Student Loans? | Bankrate

60. "Average American Household Debt in 2024: Facts and Figures", The ascent, Motely Fool, Jack Caporal, Aug 26, 2024, Average American Household Debt in 2024: Facts and Figures | The Motley Fool

61. Average US Mortgage Debt Increases to $244,498 in 2023", Experian, Chris Horymski, March 4, 2024, Average U.S. Mortgage Debt Increases to $244,498 in 2023 - Experian

62. "Einstein's 8th Wounder of the World", Clearwealth, Einstein's 8th Wonder of the World - CLEARWEALTH Asset Management

Chapter 13

63. "Snowballing vs. Stacking: Which Should You Use to Get Out of Debt", Glen Carter, Listen Money Matters, https://www.listenmoneymatters.com/get-out-of-debt-snowballing-stacking/

AUTHOR BIO

SCOTT REBER, CFP®, MBA, is the Managing Director of Reber Investments based in Denver, NC. He began his financial services career at Morgan Stanley focusing on investments and portfolio management for families, small businesses owners. In 2017 he founded Reber Investment under the umbrella of Independent Advisor Alliance, LLC and LPL Financial and opened the first office in Denver NC.

After receiving a full scholarship in baseball, he earned his Bachelor of Science degree in Computer Aided Design, Manufacturing and Analysis (CAD/CAM/CAE) from Eastern Michigan University. In 2009, he furthered his education by obtaining a Master of Business Administration degree, and in 2016, he completed the CFP® certification. He currently lives with his wife Tonya and their two children Gavin and Madelyn in the Lake Norman area of North Carolina

www.ingramcontent.com/pod-product-compliance
Lightning Source LLC
Chambersburg PA
CBHW021145130626
46554CB00005B/1675